100 PARTY COOKIES

MW00990930

NADIA KALINICHENKO AND MYRIAM SÁNCHEZ

100 PARTY COOKIES

A Step-by-Step Guide to Baking Super-Cute Cookies for Life's Little Celebrations

A QUINTET BOOK

First edition for North America and the Philippines
published in 2015 by Barron's Educational Series, Inc.

Copyright © 2015 Quintet Publishing Limited.

All rights reserved. No part of this publication may
be reproduced or distributed in any form or by any
means without the written permission of the
copyright owner.

All inquiries should be addressed to:
Barron's Educational Series, Inc.
250 Wireless Boulevard
Hauppauge, NY 11788
www.barronseduc.com

Library of Congress Control Number:
2015940222
ISBN: 978-1-4380-0729-8
QTT.TMJ

This book was designed and produced by
Quintet Publishing Limited
4th Floor, Sheridan House,
114-116 Western Road,
Hove, BN3 1DD, UK
Project Editor: Cara Frost-Sharratt
Designer: Maria Mokina
Photographer: Tony Briscoe
Art Director: Michael Charles
Editorial Director: Alana Smythe
Publisher: Mark Searle
Printed in China by 1010
987654321

*I would like to dedicate this book to my daughter Kate
who helps and supports me*

NK

In loving memory of Lilia Ontiveros (1957–2015)

MS

Contents

Introduction

Nadia

I have been fond of art since my childhood, and decorating cookies is one of my favorite hobbies. It combines my love of baking and decorating. My friends and family are my biggest critics and they enjoy trying out my creations.

I first became inspired by cookie decorating when I saw some designs on Flickr, and I immediately started to research everything I could find out about cookies on the Internet. I ordered my first 30 cookie cutters—as well as piping bags and dyes—and since then I haven't stopped baking cookies and making royal icing.

People often ask me where I get my inspiration. I find that new ideas arrive unexpectedly and inspiration can come from ordinary things— patterns on plates, fabrics, cards, toys, etc.

Some cookies could be called works of art. As with other art forms, the artist invests a lot of time and talent in their creation. However, first and foremost, a cookie must always be a cookie. That is to say, it should not only look beautiful but also taste delicious. That's why I'm a fan of simple designs with minimum use of colors.

Practice and more practice is the key to success. But always remember that at the end of the day, it's a cookie—it should be eaten and enjoyed in a few short seconds!

Nadia Kalinichenko   NK

Myriam

My love for decorated cookies began in 2007 when I first saw a simply decorated cookie while I was looking for a favor to celebrate my daughter's birthday. I am a graphic designer, so my work was not related to sugar craft in any way.

I wasn't born into a family with baking traditions, but my mother is a talented craftswoman who surprised me with everything she made. She taught me that things made with love turn out best. My husband, father, siblings and friends let me know that the support of loved ones helps you to achieve things you never thought you could. It was my eldest daughter Andy—whom we affectionately call Chapix—who started the idea that became Chapix Cookies, and both Andy and my younger daughter Lily continue to inspire me.

I had no formal training or experience in baking or decorating, but I experimented because I wanted to make my daughters happy. Suddenly, I found myself making more cookies than I expected and designing for others as well. Then in 2011, I began teaching cookie decorating classes at home and abroad.

Now I have the opportunity to share my experience in this book. There are simple designs for beginners, and more elaborate designs for those looking to improve their skills. Practice, be inspired, be patient, and—most important of all—have fun!

Myriam Sánchez   MS

Basics

Basic Recipes

SUPPLIES

- 3 cups (375 g) all-purpose flour
- 1 tsp (5 ml) baking soda
- ¼ tsp salt
- 1 egg (room temperature)
- 1 tsp (5 ml) vanilla extract
- 1 cup (225 g) unsalted butter (room temperature)
- 1 cup (200 g) sugar

Makes 20 small or 12 large cookies

TIPS

If the dough is dry, add a little butter or milk to the batter until you get a smooth dough that does not crumble.

If the dough is too greasy, add a little more flour until you get a stiff dough that does not fall apart.

Sugar Cookies

1. Sift the flour, baking soda, and salt together in a bowl and set aside.

2. Mix the egg with the vanilla extract in a small bowl and set aside.

3. Cream the butter and sugar in a mixer for about 2 minutes on medium speed, until the butter changes to a lighter tone and is smooth.

4. Add the egg and vanilla mixture and mix well. Slowly add the flour mixture to form a dough that pulls away from the bowl.

5. Wrap the dough in plastic wrap and refrigerate for at least 1 hour before cutting out.

6. Preheat the oven to 375°F (190°C). Roll out the dough on a lightly floured surface to ¼-in (½-cm) thick. Cut out the cookies using a floured cookie cutter. Place on lined baking sheets.

7. Bake in the oven for 8 to 10 minutes. Cool on a wire rack. The cookies can be kept in an airtight container for 7 to 10 days.

Variations

Chocolate

To make chocolate cookies, use the Sugar Cookie recipe, substituting ½ cup of flour with ½ cup of cocoa powder. Proceed as directed.

Citrus

Replace the vanilla extract with the equivalent amount of your favorite citrus flavor—for example, orange or lemon extract.

Gingerbread Cookies

SUPPLIES

- 3 cups (375 g) all-purpose flour
- 1 tsp (5 ml) baking soda
- 1 tsp (5 ml) ground cinnamon
- 1½ tsp (8 ml) ground ginger
- ¼ tsp (1 ml) ground allspice
- ½ cup (110 g) light brown sugar
- 4 tbsp (60 ml) molasses
- 1 egg
- ⅓ cup (75 g) melted butter

Makes 12 cookies

1. Sift the flour, baking soda, and spices together in a bowl. Add the sugar, molasses, egg, and butter and mix to a smooth dough.

2. Wrap the dough in plastic wrap and refrigerate for at least 1 hour before cutting out.

3. Preheat the oven to 375°F (190°C). Roll out the dough onto a lightly floured surface to ¼-in (½-cm) thick. Cut out the gingerbread using a floured cookie cutter. Place on lined baking sheets.

4. Bake in the oven for 8 to 10 minutes. Cool on a wire rack.

Storing and Baking Cookie Dough

STORING DOUGH

Cookie dough can be kept refrigerated for a maximum of 1 week. Frozen cookie dough can be kept for up to 3 months.

You can also freeze cutout cookies before you bake them—that way, you can prepare a number of batches and save time when you want to bake. Spread the cookies in layers in an airtight container, placing sheets of parchment paper in between each layer to prevent sticking. When you want to bake, transfer the frozen cookies directly to a cookie sheet and thaw for about 15 minutes before baking.

CUTTING COOKIES

If the dough has been frozen, you must remove it from the freezer ahead of time to reduce its hardness and make it easier to manipulate. However, dough is easier to handle when it's chilled, so avoid letting it sit at room temperature for too long, especially in warm weather. Chilled dough is easier to cut and there is less possibility that the cookies will expand during baking.

When rolling out the dough, you can roll on a lightly floured surface, or put it between two sheets of parchment paper or two good-quality, nonstick baking mats. That way, you won't need to add flour to extend the dough and so won't change the balance of the recipe.

Use cookie cutters of your choice and don't worry if you don't have the required cutter for the design—you can make your own templates by cutting out shapes from paper or acetate. Try to cut as many cookies as possible whenever you roll out the dough and avoid excessive handling, as this can change the consistency, making it brittle and difficult to handle.

BAKING TIPS

Each oven is different, so the baking time may vary depending on the size of the oven and also the size of the cookies—bigger cookies will take longer to bake, while smaller cookies will bake more quickly. You should check the cookies frequently when baking for the first time, and always bake cookies of the same size together. The basic cookie recipes in this book assume baking in a conventional gas oven. If you own a convection oven, turn the fan off or lower the temperature to avoid burning the cookies, especially the smaller decorations.

If your oven bakes cookies more quickly on one side than the other, turn the cookie sheet halfway through baking to achieve a uniform bake. After removing the cookies from the oven, leave them on the tray for 5 minutes before transferring to racks and allowing to cool completely before decorating.

STORING BAKED COOKIES

Baked cookies can be stored at room temperature or refrigerated in an airtight container that is perfectly sealed. Place the cookies in spaced layers, with sheets of parchment paper between each layer. When you are ready to decorate the cookies, remove the container from the refrigerator, but don't open it until it reaches room temperature. This will help to prevent condensation from damaging the cookies.

TIP
Decorated cookies can also be stored in the refrigerator. Keep them packed in a perfectly sealed storage bag, and keep refrigerated in an airtight container.

Royal Icing

Nearly all of the cookies in this book are decorated entirely with royal icing (except for a few details such as sprinkles). Use Myriam's recipe to achieve "Buttercream," "Meringue," "Honey," and "10-Second" consistencies, and Nadia's recipe to make royal icing with "Regular" and "Thick" consistencies (see page 14 for information on consistencies). If your brand of meringue powder contains cream of tartar, you can omit this ingredient from the recipe.

Myriam's Royal Icing Recipe

SUPPLIES

- 6 cups (750 g) sifted confectioners' sugar
- 5 tbsp (75 ml) meringue powder
- 1 tsp (5 ml) cream of tartar, if needed
- ½ cup (120 ml) water at room temperature (this should include the lemon juice)
- 2–4 tbsp natural lemon juice, strained

TIP
Before preparing royal icing ensure that all equipment is clean and free from oil (you can wipe equipment with white vinegar to remove oil).

1. Mix the dry ingredients together in the stand mixer bowl on a low speed using the paddle attachment.

2. Add the liquid and begin mixing slowly. When the ingredients are combined, mix at a medium speed for about 2 minutes.

3. The icing is ready when it reaches a dense texture that is similar to white satin buttercream.

Note: This royal icing is recommended to be prepared in a stand mixer. If you own a hand mixer, adjust the water to avoid burning out the small motor.

This recipe produces icing with a glossy finish and can be stored, in the refrigerator, for a long time.

Nadia's Royal Icing Recipe

SUPPLIES

- 5 tbsp (75 ml) meringue powder
- ½ cup (120 g) warm water
- 1 tsp (5 ml) clear vanilla
- 1 tsp (5 ml) additional flavoring (optional)
- ½ tsp (2½ ml) cream of tartar (optional)
- 3½ cups (450 g) confectioners' sugar
- 1–2 tbsp (15–30 ml) light corn syrup

TIP
To achieve the "Thick" consistency required in some of the designs, add a little more confectioners' sugar to the icing so that it is stiff enough to pipe outlines and decorations.

1. Whisk the meringue powder and warm water together in a mixing bowl for about 2 minutes.

2. Add the vanilla, additional flavoring (if using), and cream of tartar and beat for 1 minute more.

3. Gradually add the confectioners' sugar and beat on a medium speed until combined. The icing will be very thick, but that's fine, as you will add more water to the icing when mixing the colors.

4. Add the corn syrup and beat for about 1 minute.

5. Place the icing in an airtight container. Before sealing the container, cover the top of the icing with plastic wrap. Make sure the wrap is touching the icing. Store in the refrigerator until you are ready to use it.

Tools and Equipment

Making and decorating cookies requires certain essential tools and equipment. You will probably already have many of them in your own kitchen, and you can buy the rest in specialist pastry shops to gradually build your collection.

AIRTIGHT CONTAINERS

Airtight containers are essential for storing royal icing and cookies. These containers prevent the passage of air or moisture. Keep several different sizes according to your needs.

BOWLS

Bowls are indispensable for icing mixtures. Glass bowls are recommended, as this material does not store fat residues. Plastic containers can also be used, but they should be used solely for royal icing mixtures, as the material is porous and can retain fat residues so they are not appropriate for preparing icing.

COOKIE CUTTERS

What decorator doesn't love cookie cutters? They can be found in thousands of different shapes with different themes and are available in different materials—plastic, tin, stainless steel, and even copper. If you don't have a cutter to fit a particular design, you can sometimes combine different cutters to create new shapes. And simple shapes like circles, squares, rectangles, or shaped plaques can be useful for creating spectacular designs.

After each use, it is recommended that you wash cutters with soap, water, and a sponge to remove all traces of dough. To prevent stains or rusting, wipe cutters completely dry with a cloth immediately after washing. Some of the cookie cutters used in this book were custom designed by Chapix Cookies (*www.chapixcookies.com*). For more detials, see Resources on page 140.

COOKIE SHEETS

Nonstick aluminium cookie sheets are best, as there is no need to use parchment paper, so the backs of the cookies have a flat appearance. If your oven bakes cookies quickly, adjust the temperature so the cookies don't burn—thin cookie sheets conduct heat better.

COOKIE SLATS

Cookie slats are the perfect guide for rolling out cookie dough with an even thickness. They are available in plastic or wood, so it comes down to personal preference. Try to aim for cookies that are approximately ⅕–⅓-in (½–¾-cm) thick.

FONDANT SMOOTHER

While you are baking, there is a chance that your cookies will develop bumps. Don't worry about this in the middle of baking—while the cookie is still malleable you can use a pin to open a small hole in the cookie bump and release the air. You can then use a fondant smoother to remove the bump and get a flat surface. This will help when you start decorating the cookie. If you don't have a fondant smoother, you can use a large, flat spatula.

KNIFE OR X-ACTO KNIFE

When you don't own a particular cutter for a design, you can use a template to cut out the cookie shape. You will need a good knife to cut out the design by hand and the X-ACTO knife is perfect for this job.

MEASURING CUPS

Measuring cups help to measure out dry or liquid ingredients. Make sure they are completely dry and clean before every use. Measuring spoons are very useful for accurately measuring flavorings and powders.

MIXER

You can start with a hand mixer, which is perfectly adequate as long as your cookie production is small. You will need to adjust some steps when making dough and royal icing to avoid burning out the small motor, but if you end up making more cookies, or just want to ease the workload, you might consider buying a stand mixer. This has a larger bowl and a more powerful motor, which makes the preparation time quicker.

NONSTICK BAKING MATS

Nonstick baking mats can withstand very high temperatures, and they are another option for baking cookies without using flour or parchment paper to achieve a flat finish on the back of cookies.

PARCHMENT PAPER

Parchment paper is a good resource if you don't have nonstick cookie sheets. The paper will prevent the cookies from sticking to the sheet and allow faster removal of the cookies once baked. Sheets can be used several times for baking a number of batches in one day. But it is best discarded after a few uses, as it can create wrinkles in the back of the cookie. This is because the paper will gradually absorb grease and humidity after each bake.

ROLLING PIN

Rolling pins are available in different sizes and materials—wood, silicone, steel, and marble. The weight of each may vary depending on the material. Choose one that best suits your needs and that you are most comfortable using. Some rolling pins have leveling rings that help you to roll out your dough evenly. Their weak point is that they are usually short, which can limit the amount of dough that can be rolled out.

SCALES

A measuring scale is a must in every kitchen, and it is well worth investing in a good-quality scale to avoid errors. A digital scale that has dual measurement capabilities is ideal.

SPATULAS

Spatulas are some of the most useful tools when making cookie dough and royal icing, or when mixing colors. It's a good idea to have several different sizes to suit each use. Make sure to wash them thoroughly and remove all grease before using them with royal icing. Resistant spatulas are perfect for cookie dough, as they are neither too hard nor too flexible.

COMBINING COOKIE CUTTERS

There might be some designs that you would like to create but you don't have the correct cookie cutter. If this is the case, you can combine 2 or more cutters together to create the desired shape.

To do this, you need to first cut out the cookie shapes from your dough using both cutters. Next, cut away part of one shape using the other cookie cutter—this ensures the two pieces fit together exactly. So, for example, you might be creating a heart with wings and use a heart cookie cutter and a leaf-shaped cutter. For this, you would cut away a small part of each leaf so the pieces fit exactly on either side of the heart.

Lightly push the pieces together—you don't need to stick them as the heat of the oven will melt the different sections together.

Decorating Equipment and Techniques

AIRBRUSH

An airbrush is a device that is used to decorate by mixing air and paint to create gradient shades. It is a very useful tool that adds dimension and special effects to cookies.

There are simple action and double action airbrushes. Double action airbrushes offer excellent spray and definition, which means the paint won't look grainy.

Use edible airbrush colors with this device. These are thinner than food coloring, which could clog your gun. After every use, clean the gun with water or edible alcohol such as vodka. This is especially important when you use pearlescent paints.

COUPLERS

Couplers are small plastic two-part adaptors—the bigger part goes inside the piping bag and the smaller one goes outside, attaching the tip to the piping bag. Sometimes you will make different textures using the same icing, and couplers are particularly useful in these instances, as they make it easy to change tips. Some designs in the book use couplers and others don't—you will find your own preferred way of working once you have been decorating cookies for a while.

DECORATING TIPS

Piping tips are very useful when decorating cookies and you will probably build quite a collection. They are particularly useful if you need to pipe special shapes or create different textures. The most common tips in cookie decorating are rounded tips and these are often used to outline and flood cookies (see page 16). You can find them in lots of different sizes—check the number engraved on the metal.

The round tips used most for designs in this book are Nos. 1, 1.5, 2, and 3. Each is used according to the size of the work area. For piping, it is best to use the finest point. For flooding a larger area, it is better to use a bigger hole. In many of the designs, you will see a No. 1.5 tip listed, however, if you don't have this size, you can replace it with a No. 1 tip. Star-shaped tips and leaf-shaped tips are also used in a lot of designs

Piping bags

to create different textures in the cookies, such as the hair on some characters or leaves.

HEATER FAN

A fan is used to give cookies their distinctive shiny and glossy finish, and it also helps to avoid bubbling on the surface of the cookie. Turn the fan on to a medium heat for about 10 minutes.

PIPING BAGS

Piping bags are useful for decorating with royal icing. There are washable and disposable piping bags available in various sizes. The benefit of disposable piping bags is they are made of clear plastic that shows the color of the icing. They don't always need to be disposed of after a single use; some brands are such good quality that you can wash and use them several times. You will usually find them in 12 in (30 cm) size. If you feel more comfortable using a smaller bag, you can cut them to the desired length.

In addition to disposable piping bags, you can try tipless icing bags, icing bottles or parchment paper cones. You will find that some designs in the book use tips with the piping bags, while others don't. When working without tips you just have to cut off the point to the desired size and begin decorating.

PROJECTOR

If you own a projector, it can help you to speed up the cookie decorating process if you need to draw images freehand on your cookies. There are several kinds of projectors (such as Kopykake), so check the different brands and choose the one that suits you best.

SATIN RIBBON

You can add tiny ribbon bows to make cookies even cuter. There are a number of tutorials online that teach you how to make bows.

SCISSORS

You will need these to cut the tips off piping bags, and to cut parchment paper, rubber bands, plastic wrap, and other materials that you might need when decorating.

SOFT ROUND PAINTBRUSHES

You can use these to apply edible powders, such as petal dust, as they help to blend color onto the decorating surface. You will use this tool to color the cheeks of some of the characters or to create shadows on a cookie. It helps to have several sizes so you can choose the one that best suits the size of the decorating area. After each use, the brush can be cleaned using a little cornstarch; this product removes the remains of petal dust from the bristles.

SPRAY BOTTLE

Spray bottles can be found at any convenience store, and they are a great help when preparing and mixing royal icing. They provide moderate amounts of water when preparing different consistencies, which reduces the risk of adding too much water to the icing.

TEMPLATES

If you don't own a projector, another way to draw designs onto your cookies before piping is by using paper templates.

You can print the design on paper and cut out the parts that you need to trace. For example, in the Superhero Dad cookie (see page 132) you could cut out the head first, and then trace all the cookies with the same head size. After that, cut out the body and trace it, then do the same with the arms, and so on, until the design is complete.

TIES, RUBBER BANDS, OR CLIPS

Any of these products will help to close your piping bag before decorating and avoid spillage. Adjust the rubber band whenever necessary, to squeeze the icing out effortlessly.

TOOTHPICK, 2-IN-1 TOOL, SCRIBE TOOL

These three tools are very useful to help dissolve peaks, blend colors, or break air bubbles. Keep one on hand for every project.

• Toothpicks are perfect for cookie decorating beginners, as they are disposable and inexpensive. They are very useful when you work with wet-on-wet technique (see page 17). A lot of the designs in the book require blending, so you will find that you go through a lot of toothpicks. Always wipe them clean in between blending.

• The 2-in-1 tool is a plastic tool that has a pin at one end and a small shovel at the other. The shovel works perfectly to remove small amounts of excess royal icing when decorating.

• The scribe tool has a metal tip like a pin, which is very effective when trying to break a bubble in the icing.

TWEEZERS

Tweezers help to easily and accurately place sprinkles, pearls, or any other kind of small decorations on cookies.

WAX PAPER

You can use wax paper to make royal icing transfers (see page 16). It is also used for lining baking sheets and placing in between cutout cookies when freezing.

COLORS AND DECORATIONS

EDIBLE MARKERS

Edible ink markers are useful for tracing designs onto the cookie or simply to trace defined areas. They can also be used for coloring directly on dry icing. There are several brands and edge thicknesses on the market—for example, Americolor and Rainbow Dust.

It is best to use light colors to trace directly onto the cookie or onto dry royal icing. If you are marking over a dark icing shade, you will need darker colored markers.

The Rainbow Dust brand has a double-sided marker—one side is finer than the opposite side. This product is useful for drawing eyes, eyebrows, and mouths on some of the characters. Before using an edible marker, make sure the icing is completely dry, otherwise the ink could be combined with the wet icing and stain it.

If you can't find this product in your area, you can replace it with a very thin 10/0 paintbrush. Dilute black food coloring in water, clear vanilla or vodka to make the smiles and eyebrows on characters. Airbrush paint can also be used, but remember to try it first on paper before decorating your cookies.

EDIBLE PEARLS

Edible pearls come in different sizes and colors but you will most often use white and pastel colors. You should apply them on the base while it is still wet.

FOOD COLORING

Food colors are essential for coloring royal icing. They come in different presentations—liquid, gel paste, or Liqua-Gel. You should add the number of drops you need before finalizing your icing consistency, adding the color gradually, as a little goes a long way. Always choose a good-quality brand.

Food coloring that comes in a container with a dropper is best, as it is simpler and cleaner to use. Gel colors must be applied with the help of a toothpick, and should not be reintroduced to the container after touching the icing, so be sure to use a new toothpick every time.

Gel paste colors help you to mix a lot of different colors for icing. Also, by mixing them you can achieve subtly different shades in the colors. You only need a very small amount of gel paste to achieve vibrant colors, so a little goes a long way.

LUSTER DUST

Luster dust is a generic name for a group of tasteless powders, which serve to decorate cookies or cakes, to give them a touch of color and brightness. In this group you can find pearl dust, disco dust, petal dust, sparkle dust, highlighter dust, and luster dust. It is important to consider that not all are edible, even though most are labeled "non-toxic." Check your local laws, as some colors may be approved in one country but not in another. Using any of these products is optional.

A lot of the designs in the book include petal dust to decorate the cheeks of characters or to shade specific areas. When used for cheeks, you can choose the tone of your choice but it is best to opt for a medium pink tone.

To apply petal dust, take a very small amount of the dust with the tip of a paintbrush—if you take it from the lid or the walls of the container, you know that you won't exceed the amount. Remove any excess dust by shaking the brush or by using a paper towel, and apply gradually to the icing in a circular motion. If the color you chose is a light tone, you might need to repeat the process until you reach the desired tone.

METALLIC FOOD PAINT

You need a dry paintbrush to use this paint. To achieve a good result, do not add any water to the paint and apply another coat, if needed, once the first coat has dried on the cookie.

SPRINKLES

A lot of cookie designs include sprinkles, pearls, dragees, and nonpareils. Their different shapes and colors help to create unique designs, and the right finishing touches can increase the visual appeal of each cookie. Add these decorations to the cookie while the icing is wet, using accent tweezers to apply, so that your fingers don't touch the icing.

ROYAL ICING

Royal icing is a very versatile medium for decorating. With it, you can create simple or very complex designs using a few basic decorating techniques. Mastering royal icing requires practice and patience, as it takes time to learn how to prepare and handle it. Practice every day until you get the desired results and you feel confident enough to try out some designs on cookies.

CONSISTENCIES

To create different decorative effects, volume, and textures with royal icing, you can work with consistencies. The consistencies are achieved by thinning the icing with water. You will notice the different methods used by the authors in the book, but each project is clearly labelled with the consistency alongside the icing color.

Consistencies 1–3 below are likened to an ingredient you will know or recognize. It is helpful to think of those products while adding water. The amount of water is crucial, but variable, depending on climate, temperature, and brand of ingredients. Use a spray bottle to add water to the icing, as too much or too little will mean the icing will not work as desired.

1. BUTTERCREAM CONSISTENCY (MYRIAM)

This has little water and has the appearance of buttercream. It is a firm consistency, but it must flow through the tip without effort and it has to stick on the cookie. It is used to make textures that keep the piping tip shape—for example, leaves, flowers, hair, etc.

2. MERINGUE CONSISTENCY (MYRIAM)

This consistency has increased water content and, therefore, has a creamy appearance. It is useful for piping decorations with volume, such as character faces. It is also perfect for outlining and writing.

3. HONEY CONSISTENCY (MYRIAM)

This is visually similar to a dense honey. It is suitable for flooding cookies with an invisible outline. It's a 2-in-1 consistency, which means it is easy to outline and flood at the same time, while retaining its volume.

4. 10-SECOND CONSISTENCY (MYRIAM)

This consistency is the best known in the cookie decorating world and it works exactly as its name indicates. To prepare it, add water until you can cut a line on the icing with a knife; the line must disappear in 10 seconds. This consistency is fluid and perfect for flooding cookies flat. With this icing, it is best to outline the cookie first to prevent spillage. It is useful when working with the wet-on-wet technique (see page 17).

5. REGULAR (NADIA)

This is an "in between" consistency. That means the icing should be thick enough to hold piped lines but thin enough to flood the cookie.

6. THICK (NADIA)

To achieve a thick consistency for detailed piping work and outlining, keep the icing very stiff and don't add any extra water.

COLORING

Because royal icing needs water to make different consistencies, the sugar will melt with the passing hours. It is therefore best to prepare colors in their required consistencies just before using them.

It is best—but not essential—to prepare dark colors like black, brown, and red in advance. Some colors tend to increase by a shade a few hours later, so it's possible that you could saturate the royal icing and change its flavor and consistency. For black icing, you should reach the black shade gradually, working toward gray first, and then waiting a few hours to see how much the shade has darkened before adding more food coloring. Always taste the icing before you use it, to avoid bitterness—the cookie needs to taste great and look great!

STORAGE

When kept at room temperature, the useful period of icing for decorative purposes is 1 week. After that, it will gradually lose its ability to dry hard. So, royal icing is best stored in an airtight container in the refrigerator, where it will last for up to 1 month. Place plastic wrap on the icing surface to prevent a crust from forming.

When using refrigerated icing, remove it from the refrigerator ahead of time and allow it to come to room temperature before using. This helps it to reach the right consistency for decoration.

Icing gets diluted while resting, especially if it contains a lot of water. So, before using it, mix it again to check the consistency—you can adjust it by adding some confectioners' sugar to restore the desired consistency, or add water to dilute it.

If you need to work with white icing that has been resting, mix it again to restore the original color. If necessary, add white food coloring to prevent it from becoming yellow when it dries.

DECORATING TECHNIQUES

AIRBRUSHING

Before starting, carefully choose an area where you will work with the airbrush—preferably a wide area that won't be affected by spray paint. You can use a cardboard box for this purpose.

When you decorate gradient edges, consider the distance between the gun and the cookie—too close creates a thin line, but too far away could result in covering the whole cookie surface and the effect will be lost. A distance of about 2 in (5 cm) is about right, depending on the size of the cookie.

When you are airbrushing around cookies, you can put the cookie on a turntable or paper towel. Turn it while you work so you can move the cookie without touching it. Try not to apply too much paint, as it can take a long time to dry. If you do, you can dry it in the oven. You don't have to own an airbrush to create three-dimensional effects; you can use petal dust in small areas (see Luster Dust).

DRYING TECHNIQUES

Many of the cookies in this book are decorated in layers—several details added at the same time. The important thing to remember when using this method is that adjacent details are never added at the same time. To master this method it is helpful to know about drying techniques.

Royal icing dries quickly in hot and dry weather. If you live in an area like this, your icing will dry very quickly, and it will have a beautiful shiny surface that is free from craters and sinkings. However, if you live in a humid area, you will need the help of a drying method to speed up your decorating process and increase the chances of successful results. One option is to dry the icing in your oven. Turn it on until it reaches a temperature of 122°F (50°C) then turn it off. Put the cookies on a cookie sheet and place in the oven until it cools. You can repeat the process, but don't exceed the temperature.

Another option is a dehumidifier. This device absorbs moisture from your working space, which helps to speed up the drying process. This method is recommended if you normally work in sugar craft and need a dry environment all the time. There are several brands and sizes, so choose the option that suits you.

If your cookie production is small, another option is a food dehydrator—there are several brands and models on the market. It is advisable to purchase one that has a temperature regulator to control the heat and to avoid damage to your decorations. These are not the only options to dry royal icing—there are others such as a fan, a heat fan, a heat gun, or a lamp, among others.

FLOODING

Flooding is a basic technique to fill previously outlined areas; usually using thin icing that helps to achieve an even surface. It is a common technique but is mostly used to decorate larger areas or to decorate with the wet-on-wet technique (see page 17).

INVISIBLE OUTLINES

To make invisible outlines, outline and flood immediately using the same icing consistency. Shake the piping tip over the icing until the icing gets an even surface. To get an even surface, fix with a toothpick or scribe tool.

LEAVES

Using a leaf tip or rounded tip, place the piping bag at a 45-degree angle. Press the icing close to the flower (if included) to pipe a dot. While piping, gradually reduce the pressure until you achieve a leaf shape.

OUTLINING

Outlining is an essential technique to master when you begin your cookie journey. It helps to define the areas to be decorated and to create a barrier that prevents icing spills and unwanted blending when you are decorating using a thin consistency. Rounded piping tips are best for piping an outline.

PAINTING ON A COOKIE

Before painting, make sure the cookies are completely dry by leaving them overnight. You should also practice painting designs on paper before working on cookies. When you are ready to paint your cookies, choose a good selection of brushes, including some that are very thin. Put drops of the colors you will be using in the palette. Dip the brush in water then drag it across a paper towel to remove the excess water (the icing should not have any drops of water on it). After that you can start using colors.

For pastel and lighter colors just add a little white food coloring to regular colors. Don't be afraid to start painting on cookies even if you have never done it before; just begin with the simplest details and patterns.

PIPING

Piping is a technique that will require practice and patience, and it's very important to use the right icing consistency. Meringue is a good choice, as it's an elastic consistency that holds its shape.

If you have never piped before, practice piping straight lines on parchment paper. Gently press the icing bag until you see a tiny drop on the tip. Touch the tip to the surface you are decorating. Lift the piping bag off, squeezing with an even pressure, to make straight lines from the left to the right side. Guide the royal icing where you need to and let gravity help you. If you drag the icing right onto the cookie the lines won't look even.

Piping and flooding

To pipe swirl lines, you use almost the same technique—when you lift the piping bag up (keeping it straight at 90 degrees), guide the icing where you need it. Don't drag it; just very gently place it, as if you were releasing a ribbon.

ROYAL ICING TRANSFERS

Royal icing transfers are decorative pieces of icing that are made in advance to speed up the decoration process. To make them, you'll need a cookie sheet, a template with the necessary image, and wax paper. Using masking tape, attach the template to the cookie sheet and cover the template with a wax paper sheet. Make sure it is wax-side up to make it easier to peel off the transfers with the help of a spatula once you have piped over the template.

Let the transfers dry completely before you very carefully peel them off. Store them in an airtight container to keep them away from moisture. If you are using transfers made prior to your last project, make sure they are still fresh before using them as a decoration.

TRANSFER EYES You can pipe these freehand, but if you feel more comfortable making all your eyes to exactly the same size, you can make a template with circles ⅕-in (½-cm) diameter as a guide, and place on the wax paper. Pipe a white dot, followed by a smaller black dot for the pupil.

FACES For a full face shape, use meringue consistency, tan royal icing. Pipe a spiral onto the wax paper until a circle is formed. Gradually fill with icing until the face is round. To get an even surface, shake the piping tip as you work.

FACE FEATURES Make a template by tracing a ¾-in (2-cm) diameter circle and adding the features you require (eyes, mouth, etc). Attach the template to the cookie sheet, cover with wax paper, and pipe as many faces as you need. Allow to dry completely (about 8 hours).

ROYAL ICING FLOWERS These are used in a lot of designs. To make them, you will need the icing color of your choice in buttercream consistency, a No. 107 tip, and white edible pearls. Position the piping bag at 90 degrees, close to the wax paper. Squeeze the piping bag and make a flower shape, then release the pressure and remove the piping bag. While the icing is wet, use accent tweezers to add an edible pearl in the center of the flower.

STAMPING

There are beautiful stamp designs on the market that are cling-mounted on wooden or acrylic blocks. The acrylic ones have the advantage of being transparent, so they help you to see the exact place you're stamping the cookie.

Outline and flood the cookie using the color icing of your choice and allow to dry for about 24 hours. The icing must be perfectly dry and preferably with an even surface so the stamp is complete. Use edible ink to stamp cookies. This could be edible airbrush paint or food coloring diluted with edible alcohol, such as vodka. Alcohol helps to speed up the drying process.

You can use a foam roller to apply ink on the stamp, but you could also use a sponge, a foam brush, or any tool that helps you to apply the ink on your stamp evenly. Before stamping your cookie, practice

Wet-on-wet technique

on parchment paper. When you are confident stamping, you can move onto your cookies. Press gently to apply the stamp evenly onto the surface. Release the pressure and remove the stamp from the cookie. Allow to dry.

SWIRL ROSES

To make a swirl rose you need to use a dense royal icing consistency like buttercream. Using a round or star piping tip, position the piping bag at a 90-degree angle, close to the cookie. Squeeze the piping bag, and make a point at the center of what will be the rose. Maintain pressure while making a spiral around the point to the desired diameter. Without releasing the pressure, continue to spiral inward, downsizing and ending at the center of the flower.

WET-ON-DRY

This technique is used to make lines or details that have volume. Icing can sometimes achieve a thin crust in a few minutes, and this is all you need to add new details that won't blend into the icing on the base. You basically add more details to the previously piped or flooded icing once it has formed a crust.

WET-ON-WET

The main feature of this technique is to create flat visual effects combining two or more icing colors in the same thin consistency. To create this effect, use 10-second consistency, and add details to previously piped or flooded icing while it is still wet. It is important to work quickly so the icing doesn't form a crust before you finish.

BIRTHDAY PARTIES

First Birthday

Baby's first birthday is one of the most memorable, and these cute little cookie favors will make sure you celebrate in style. I use pink icing here but you can personalize your cookies with the pastel icing shade of your preference. *MS*

SUPPLIES

- First birthday cookie cutter
- Yellow edible marker
- 6 piping bags and couplers
- Piping tips (Nos. 1.5, 2, 3, 14)
- White edible glitter
- Round No. 4 or No. 5 paintbrush
- Pink petal dust
- Accent tweezers
- Multicolored nonpareils
- Fine black edible marker
- Toothpick
- White edible airbrush color
- Royal icing:

White (honey consistency)

Pastel pink (meringue consistency)

White (buttercream consistency)

Pastel blue (meringue consistency)

Flesh (meringue consistency)

Light brown (meringue consistency)

1

Choose a basic cookie recipe on page 7, and make a batch of cookies using a first birthday cutter. Allow the cookies to cool completely before decorating. Use a yellow edible marker to trace the division between the hat, the number one, and the baby. Outline and flood the number one using white icing (honey consistency) and No. 3 tip. Outline and flood the hat using pink icing and No. 2 tip. Allow to dry completely.

2

Pipe a zigzag line at the bottom of the hat, using white icing (buttercream consistency) and No. 14 tip. While the icing is wet, pour white edible glitter over the zigzag. Pipe a swirl on top of the hat with the same icing and tip. Add edible glitter to the swirl. Pipe small dots on the hat using blue icing and No. 1.5 tip. Pipe the baby's head on the bottom of the number one using flesh icing and No. 2 tip. Allow to dry completely.

3

Using a paintbrush, apply pink petal dust on the cheeks. Pipe the baby's hair using light brown icing and No. 1.5 tip. Pipe the baby's pacifier using pink icing and No. 1.5 tip. While the icing is wet, use accent tweezers to add a white nonpareil in the middle. Use a fine black edible marker to draw eyes.

4

Dip a toothpick in white edible airbrush color and paint a small dot on each cheek. Pipe slanted lines across the cookie using white icing (honey consistency) and No. 2 tip. While the icing is wet, quickly pour multicolored nonpareils over the lines.

Balloon

Balloons mean parties! This simple design uses wet-on-wet technique (see page 17), so you will have to work fast to lay down all the details before the icing forms a crust. *MS*

SUPPLIES

- Balloon cookie cutter
- 4 piping bags and couplers
- Piping tips (Nos. 1.5, 2, 3)
- Accent tweezers
- White star sprinkles
- Royal icing (honey consistency):
  Lime green
  Orange
  Teal
  White

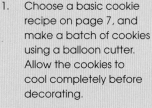

1. Choose a basic cookie recipe on page 7, and make a batch of cookies using a balloon cutter. Allow the cookies to cool completely before decorating.

2. Outline and flood the cookie (except the knot) using the icing color of your choice (I use lime green, orange and teal for my cookies) and No. 3 tip.

3. While the icing is wet, pipe an oval shape on the top left corner of the cookie using white icing and No. 2 tip. Pipe a small dot just above the oval. Pipe a short line on the bottom right corner of the balloon for a reflection.

4. While the icing is wet, use accent tweezers to add 3 star sprinkles to the balloon. Allow to dry completely.

5. Pipe the balloon knot using the same color icing and No. 1.5 tip. (To avoid craters, you can accelerate the drying process with the drying tool of your choice—see page 15.)

Ice Cream Cone

This type of novelty cookie is loved by kids and adults alike. I add sprinkles to make the ice cream look as realistic as possible—you can choose whichever color you like for these decorations. *NK*

SUPPLIES

- Ice cream cone cookie cutter
- 3 piping bags
- Sprinkles
- Royal icing:
  Ivory (thick consistency)
  White (regular consistency)
  Ivory (regular consistency)

1

Choose a basic cookie recipe on page 7, and make a batch of cookies using an ice cream cone cutter. Allow the cookies to cool completely before decorating. Prepare the piping bags by cutting a 1–2-mm hole for piping and a 3-mm hole for flooding. Outline the cone with ivory icing (thick consistency) and the top with white icing.

2

Flood the ice cream cone with ivory icing (regular consistency) and flood the top of the ice cream with white icing. While the icing is wet, add sprinkles on top.

3

Pipe lines on the cone using ivory icing (thick consistency). Allow to dry completely.

4

Flood the remaining ice cream section with white icing, allowing a little to drip down over the top of the cone, as if the ice cream is beginning to melt.

Basketball

Who doesn't love easy cookies? This basketball is very simple to make but still looks amazing thanks to the effects of airbrushing. *MS*

SUPPLIES

- 2¾-in (7-cm) round cookie cutter
- 2 piping bags and couplers
  - Piping tips (Nos. 1.5, 3)
  - Airbrush
- Orange edible airbrush color
- Fine black edible marker
- Royal icing:
  Light orange (honey consistency)
  Black (meringue consistency)

1. Choose a basic cookie recipe on page 7, and make a batch of cookies using a round cutter. Allow the cookies to cool completely before decorating.

2. Outline and flood the cookie using light orange icing and No. 3 tip. Allow to dry completely.

3. Airbrush the ball edges using orange edible airbrush color. Allow to dry completely.

4. Trace the ball ribs using a black edible marker and the provided template (see pages 134–139). Pipe over the ribs using black icing and No. 1.5 tip.

5. Pipe 3 dots onto the cookie using orange icing and No. 1.5 tip.

Soccer Ball

The volume technique is the best way to create a realistic quilted look. You can adapt this cookie for your little champ's favorite sport or use their team colors to make the cookies even more personal. *MS*

SUPPLIES

- 3½-in (9-cm) round cookie cutter
- Brown edible marker
- 2 piping bags and couplers
  - Piping tip (No. 2)
- Royal icing (meringue consistency):
  Black
  White

TIPS & TRICKS

Drying is key to achieving a realistic effect with this cookie. Each segment must be dry before filling the next to ensure the divisions are distinct.

Choose a basic cookie recipe on page 7, and make a batch of cookies using a round cutter. Allow the cookies to cool completely before decorating. Using a brown edible marker, trace the soccer ball pattern using the provided template (see pages 134–139) or a projector. Next, outline and fill the center black pentagon and the outer black pentagons using black icing and No. 2 tip. Allow to dry.

Using the picture as a guide, outline and fill each hexagon using white icing and No. 2 tip.

To get a quilted look you need to be careful not to outline and fill adjacent shapes at the same time.

Let each shape dry completely before filling the next one.

Superhero

Superheroes are a popular theme for children's parties. This cute, little character has been designed to recreate comics by using a simple outlined decorating technique. This project requires care to fill each area, so I use small, round decorating tips. *MS*

SUPPLIES

- Superhero cookie cutter
- Yellow edible marker
- 7 piping bags and couplers
- Piping tips (Nos. 1.5, 2)
- Fine black edible marker
- Round No. 4 or No. 5 paintbrush
- Pink petal dust
- Toothpick
- White edible airbrush color
- Royal icing (honey consistency):
  Black
  Flesh
  Brown
  Royal blue
  Super red
  White
  Yellow

1

Choose a basic cookie recipe on page 7, and make a batch of cookies using a superhero cutter. Allow the cookies to cool completely before decorating. Trace the superhero drawing onto the cookie with a yellow edible marker. Outline the character using black icing and No. 1.5 tip. Allow to dry completely.

2

Flood the head using flesh icing and No. 2 tip. Change the tip to No. 1.5 and fill the hands and legs.

3

Flood the hair using brown icing and No. 1.5 tip. Flood the body using royal blue icing and No. 1.5 tip.

6

Fill the mask in royal blue icing. Immediately pipe 2 white dots for the whites of the eyes. Next, pipe 2 black dots for pupils, and, finally, 2 white smaller dots for reflections (see picture). Fill the exclamation mark using yellow icing and No. 1.5 tip. Using a paintbrush, apply pink petal dust to the cheeks. Dip the toothpick in white edible airbrush color and paint a dot on each cheek. Draw a smile using the black marker.

4

Flood the arms and boots using super red icing and No. 1.5 tip. While the icing is wet, pipe 1 short white icing line onto each boot for reflections using No. 1.5 tip.

5

Trace the mask onto the face and the exclamation mark onto the body using a black edible marker. Outline with black icing and No. 1.5 tip. Fill the cape using yellow icing and No. 1.5 tip.

Pirate

Ahoy there! If you are thinking of hosting a pirate party, this little guy could be a great treat. This cookie is decorated in bold, friendly colors, but you can vary the colors according to your event. *MS*

SUPPLIES

- Pirate cookie cutter
- 6 piping bags and couplers
- Brown edible marker
- Piping tips (Nos. 1.5, 3, 5, 14)
- Accent tweezers
- Black edible pearls (4 mm)
- Round No. 4 or No. 5 paintbrush
- Pink petal dust
- Toothpick
- White edible airbrush color
- Fine black edible marker
- Royal icing:

Flesh (honey consistency)

Navy blue (honey consistency)

Egg yellow (meringue consistency)

White (meringue consistency)

Super red (meringue consistency)

Brown (buttercream consistency)

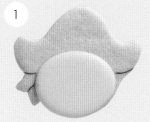

1

Choose a basic cookie recipe on page 7, and make a batch of cookies using a pirate cutter. Allow the cookies to cool completely before decorating. Trace the hat, face, and bandana areas using a brown edible marker and the provided template (see pages 134–139). Outline and flood the face using flesh icing and No. 3 tip. Allow to dry.

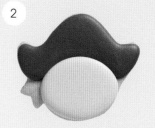

2

Outline and flood the hat using navy blue icing and No. 3 tip. Allow to dry.

3

Pipe a line on the upper edge of the hat using egg yellow icing and No. 5 tip. Outline and fill the skull using white icing and No. 1.5 tip. While the icing is wet, use tweezers to add 2 black edible pearls as eyes. Pipe the red knot using super red icing and No. 1.5 tip. Pipe the right ear using flesh icing and No. 1.5 tip.

4

Pipe the bandana using super red icing and No. 1.5 tip. While the icing is wet, pipe white dots on the bandana using No. 1.5 tip. Pipe the upper tie, and pipe white dots on the tie. Use white icing and No. 1.5 tip to pipe the skull bones.

5

Pipe the bandana's lower tie end using the same icing and tip. While the icing is wet, pipe white dots onto the tie. Make the bang by piping 4 lines beside the bandana using brown icing and No. 14 tip.

6

Using a paintbrush, apply pink petal dust to the cheeks. Dip the toothpick in white edible airbrush color and paint a small dot on each cheek. Draw the eyebrows, eyes, and smile on the pirate's face, and a smile on the skull, using a black edible marker and the picture as a guide.

Rocket

Many kids dream about traveling to space, and these colorful cookie rockets will make a fantastic centerpiece for a space-themed party. There's a lot of different icing colors and decorations for this design, so the key to success is good organization. *MS*

SUPPLIES

- Space cookie cutter
- Yellow edible marker
- 6 piping bags and couplers
- Piping tips (Nos. 1.5, 2, 3, 13 or 14 star tip)
- Accent tweezers
- Yellow star sprinkles
- Yellow edible glitter
- Round No. 4 or No. 5 paintbrush
- Pink petal dust
- Fine black edible marker
- Toothpick
- White edible airbrush color
- Royal icing:

  White (meringue consistency)

  Egg yellow (honey consistency)

  Super red (honey consistency)

  Royal blue (honey consistency)

  Flesh (meringue consistency)

  Brown (buttercream consistency)

TIPS & TRICKS

To pipe even dots, squeeze and apply the same hand pressure every time. Practice on paper before decorating cookies.

1. Choose a basic cookie recipe on page 7, and make a batch of cookies using a space cutter. Allow the cookies to cool completely before decorating. Trace the divisions onto the rocket using a yellow edible marker. Outline the rocket using white icing and No. 1.5 tip. Do not outline the central divisions.

2. The rocket body uses the wet-on-wet technique (see page 17), so try to work fast and apply the three colors before the icing forms a crust. Flood the rocket nose using egg yellow icing and No. 1.5 tip. Immediately flood the body using super red icing and No. 1.5 tip. Next, pipe the rocket base using royal blue icing and No. 1 tip. Allow to dry.

3. When the rocket is completely dry, pipe the face using flesh icing and No. 2 tip. Pipe the rocket wings one at a time, using royal blue icing and No. 1.5 tip. While the icing is wet, use tweezers to add a yellow star sprinkle on the bottom of each wing. Next, pipe the inner flame using red icing and No. 1.5 tip. Next to it, pipe the egg yellow icing to combine. While the icing is wet, apply edible glitter. Allow to dry.

4. Use a No. 4 or No. 5 paintbrush to apply pink petal dust to the face. Carefully pipe a yellow ring around the face using yellow icing and No. 3 tip. Pipe smaller dots as rivets on the rocket using blue and super red icing and No. 1.5 tip. Pipe small red dots around each yellow star (see picture).

5. When the yellow ring is dry, draw eyes and a smile using a fine black edible marker. Dip the toothpick in white edible airbrush color and paint a small dot on each cheek. Pipe small dots as rivets in yellow icing around the yellow ring, using No. 1.5 tip. Next, add blue dots using No. 1.5 tip (see picture). Pipe 3 yellow icing dots on the base of the rocket using No. 1.5 tip. Finally, pipe the kid's bang onto the top of the head. Very carefully press, pull, and release, using brown icing and No. 13 or 14 star tip.

Ballerina

This pretty, little dancer will be the talking point of your own ballerina's birthday party. There are a lot of small details on these cookies, but if you take your time and allow the icing to dry in between each application, you will achieve the desired effect. MS

SUPPLIES

- 4-in (10-cm) fluted edge circle cookie cutter
- Smaller round cookie cutter
- Yellow edible marker
- 5 piping bags and couplers
- Piping tips (Nos. 1.5, 2, 3, 14)
- Silver edible marker
- White edible glitter
- Accent tweezers
- Mini gold dragees
- Round No. 4 or No. 5 paintbrush
- Pink petal dust
- Toothpick
- White edible airbrush color
- Fine black edible marker
- Royal icing:
  White (honey consistency)
  Flesh (meringue consistency)
  Pink (meringue consistency)
  Pink (buttercream consistency)
  Brown (buttercream consistency)

1

Choose a basic cookie recipe on page 7, and make a batch of cookies using a fluted edge circle cutter. Allow the cookies to cool completely before decorating. Using a smaller round cutter and a yellow edible marker, mark a circle on the cookie. Outline and flood the circle using white icing and No. 3 tip. Allow to dry completely. Trace the ballerina drawing, using a silver edible marker, onto the white icing. Use the provided template (see pages 134–139).

2

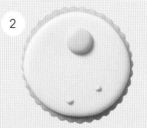

Pipe the face using flesh icing and No. 2 tip. Pipe the pointe shoes using pink icing and No. 1.5 tip.

3

Pipe the body using pink icing and No. 1.5 tip. Pipe the legs using flesh icing and No. 1.5 tip.

4

Pipe the arms using flesh icing and No. 1.5 tip. Then, pipe the tutu in a zigzag using pink icing (buttercream consistency) and No. 14 tip. While the icing is wet, add white edible glitter.

5

Pipe a star on the chest with pink icing (buttercream consistency) and No.14 tip. While the icing is wet, use tweezers to add a gold dragee in the center of the star. For the hair, pipe a spiral on the face, starting from the middle of the head, using brown icing and No. 14 tip. Pipe a second spiral on the opposite side. Pipe a third spiral around the top of the head. While the icing is wet, add 3 mini gold dragees in the center of the hair. Pipe pink dots around the fluted edge using pink icing (meringue consistency) and No. 2 tip (see picture). Allow to dry.

6

Use a paintbrush to apply pink petal dust to the cheeks. Dip the toothpick in white edible airbrush color and paint a dot on each cheek. Draw eyes, a smile, and eyebrows using a black edible marker. On the fluted edge, pipe white dots with No. 1.5 tip. Allow to dry.

MERMAID

Mermaids are the most beautiful creatures in fairy tales. I love making mermaid cookies, as they are always popular at parties. This cute, little character has been decorated in classic colors, but you can create any color combination to suit your theme. *MS*

SUPPLIES

- Mermaid cookie cutter
- Yellow edible marker
- 6 piping bags and couplers
  - Piping tips (Nos. 1.5, 2, 3)
  - Pink flower sprinkles
  - Round No. 4 or No. 5 paintbrush
  - Pink petal dust
  - Toothpick
- White edible airbrush color
- Fine black edible marker
  - Royal icing:

Flesh (meringue consistency)

Light, medium, and dark teal (honey consistency)

Light and medium orange (honey consistency)

TIPS & TRICKS

Use a toothpick or scribe tool to help merge the lines in different shades onto the tail, tail fin, and hair.

1. Choose a basic cookie recipe on page 7, and make a batch of cookies using a mermaid cutter. Allow the cookies to cool completely before decorating. Draw the mermaid outline on the cookie with a yellow edible marker.

2. Outline and flood the face using flesh icing and No. 3 tip. Outline and flood the tail using medium teal icing and No. 2 tip. While the icing is wet, pipe a curved line on the right side of the hip using light teal icing and No. 1.5 tip (see picture). Pipe another line on the opposite side using dark teal icing and No. 1.5 tip. Pipe groups of 3 dots in different areas of the tail with light teal icing and No. 1.5 tip. Allow to dry completely.

3. Outline and flood the pony tail using medium orange icing and No. 2 tip. While the icing is wet, pipe a line in light orange icing on the lower hair area using No. 1.5 tip. Outline and flood the torso with flesh icing and No. 1.5 tip. While the icing is wet, add 2 pink flower sprinkles on the torso. Outline and flood the tail fin near the cookie edge using light teal icing and No. 1.5 tip. Pipe 3 lines using medium teal icing and No. 1 tip (see picture). Allow to dry.

4. Outline and flood the left bang using orange icing and No. 1.5 tip. Outline and flood the arms using flesh icing and No. 1.5 tip.

5. Outline and flood the second bang using the same icing and tip. Outline and flood the second tail fin using the same technique, color, and tip. To decorate the pelvic fin, use light teal icing and No. 1.5 tip. Hold the piping bag at a 90-degree angle, and pipe a drop—start in the middle, pull down, and fill the end. Pipe 3 equal smaller dots at each side of the drop, trying not to blend.

6. Use a paintbrush to apply pink petal dust on the cheeks. Dip the toothpick in white edible airbrush color and paint a small dot on each cheek. Draw eyes, eyelashes, and a smile using a black edible marker. As a final detail, add 1 light teal icing dot in each pink flower sprinkle.

Princess

I like making a fluffy dress for my cookie princess, so I use wavy lines and lots of bright colors. I combine tulip and heart cookie cutters to form the main shape, as more people are likely to have these in their cutter collection. *NK*

SUPPLIES

- Tulip cookie cutter
- Heart cookie cutter
- 9 piping bags
- Metal skewer
- Paintbrush or cotton swab
- Flamingo blossom dust
- Royal icing (regular consistency):

  Pink

  Fuchsia

  Violet

  White

  Tan

  Black

  Red

  Brown

  Yellow

1. Choose a basic cookie recipe on page 7, and make a batch of cookies using tulip and heart cutters. Before baking, turn the tulips upside down and stick them to the hearts to create princess shapes. Allow the cookies to cool completely before decorating. Prepare the piping bags by cutting a 1–2-mm hole for piping and a 3-mm hole for flooding.

2. Outline and flood the lower section of the skirt with pink icing. Using fuchsia icing, pipe the upper layer of the skirt. Pipe 2 vertical lines with fuchsia icing, working from top to bottom.

3. Pipe the corset with pink icing. Pipe the upper parts of the sleeves with violet icing. Allow to dry completely.

4. Pipe the middle parts of the sleeves with violet icing and allow to dry.

5. Pipe the collar and the second layer of the skirt with white icing. Pipe the bottom part of the sleeves with violet icing. Pipe the neck and hands with tan icing.

6. Pipe the crossed lines for the corset using pink icing. Pipe the wavy line on the bottom of the skirt with fuchsia icing.

7. Pipe the head with tan icing. While wet, pipe the eyes with black icing. Using a metal skewer, drag it up from the eye to make eyelashes. Use the skewer and black icing to draw the brows. Pipe the lips with red icing. Drag the skewer through the lips to make a smile.

8. Outline the collar and white layer of the skirt with white icing and pipe the ruffles on the sleeves.

9. Use brown icing to pipe the hair and make curls. Use yellow icing to pipe the crown. Using a paintbrush or cotton swab, paint flamingo blossom dust on the cheeks. Allow to dry completely.

Dinosaur

Who doesn't love a dinosaur? This cheerful guy will appeal to cookie lovers of all ages. If you are feeling adventurous and have some extra time, you can create a menagerie of dinosaurs and vary the design for each one. *MS*

SUPPLIES

- 3½-in (9-cm) round cookie cutter
- 5 piping bags and couplers
- Piping tips (Nos. 1.5, 2, 3, 65 leaf tip)
- Yellow edible marker
  - Black edible nonpareils
- Round No. 4 or No. 5 paintbrush
  - Blue petal dust
  - Fine black edible marker
  - Royal icing:
    Teal (honey consistency)
    Light and medium orange (honey consistency)
    White (meringue consistency)
    Lime green (buttercream consistency)

1 Choose a basic cookie recipe on page 7, and make a batch of cookies using a round cutter. Allow the cookies to cool completely before decorating. Outline and flood the cookie using teal icing and No. 3 tip. Allow to dry completely. Trace the dinosaur, using a yellow edible marker and the provided template (see pages 134–139).

2 Outline and flood the dinosaur using medium orange icing and No. 2 tip. Immediately, add dots to the back and hooves using light orange icing and No. 1.5 tip. While the icing is wet, add black edible nonpareils as eyes—you will need to work fast. Using white icing and No. 2 tip, pipe 4 adjacent dots to make a fluffy cloud.

3 Pipe the grass using lime green icing and No. 65 leaf tip.

4 Add 2 smaller clouds, if desired. Allow to dry. Use a paintbrush to apply blue petal dust to the cloud intersections and around the edge of the cookie. Draw a smile using a fine black edible marker. Allow to dry.

TIPS & TRICKS

You can substitute the black edible nonpareils by piping black royal icing dots using No. 1.5 tip. Make sure the dinosaur is completely dry before piping to avoid bleeding.

Pony

Ponies are another popular choice for animal lovers' parties, and this little character will put a smile on everyone's face. This design uses the airbrush technique (see page 15), so it's worth practicing on paper before you decorate your cookies. *NK*

SUPPLIES

- Pony cookie cutter
- 8 piping bags
- Airbrush
- Brown edible airbrush color
- Toothpick
- Royal icing (regular consistency):
  - Brown
  - Gold
  - White
  - Black
  - Tan
  - Red
  - Blue
  - Yellow

1

Choose a basic cookie recipe on page 7, and make a batch of cookies using a pony cutter. Allow the cookies to cool completely before decorating. Prepare the piping bags by cutting a 1–2-mm hole for piping and a 3-mm hole for flooding. Outline and flood the pony's body with brown icing, leaving out the ear and muzzle.

2

While the icing is wet, pipe dots on the back using gold icing. Pipe a white dot then a black dot in for the eye. Using a toothpick, drag through the dot to create the eye detail. Pipe the ear and muzzle with tan icing. While the icing is wet, pipe a brown dot on the muzzle. Pipe the hooves using black icing.

3

Pipe the saddle with red and blue icing. Pipe the bow with red icing. Then outline the body and pipe the tail and crest with brown icing.

4

Using an airbrush and brown airbrush food color, airbrush a shadow around the outline of the pony. Outline the bow and the blue part of the saddle with red icing. Pipe yellow dots around the saddle. Pipe a line above the eye using brown icing. Allow to dry completely.

Numbers

I use sweet sixteen as my inspiration for this cookie. If you are a beginner, this design is perfect to practice basic cookie decorating techniques. *MS*

SUPPLIES

- Number cookie cutter
- 3 piping bags and couplers
- Piping tips (Nos. 1.5, 3)
- Pink edible glitter
- Royal icing (honey consistency):
  Electric pink
  Black
  White

TIPS & TRICKS

I use Wilton number cookie cutters. If you are decorating bigger numbers it might be necessary to change the honey consistency to 10-second consistency when flooding the cookie.

1. Choose a basic cookie recipe on page 7, and make a batch of cookies using a number cutter. Allow the cookies to cool completely before decorating.

2. Outline the number using electric pink icing and No. 1.5 tip. Allow to dry.

3. Change to No. 3 tip and flood the number using the same icing.

4. While the icing is wet, pipe some polka dots using black and white icing.

5. While the icing is wet, pour pink edible glitter over the cookie. Allow to dry completely.

Butterfly

This pretty butterfly cookie is bursting with bright, summery colors and lots of decorations on the wings. The face really brings it to life, so take your time creating realistic features with the edible marker. *MS*

SUPPLIES

- Butterfly cookie cutter
- Yellow edible marker
- 5 piping bags and couplers
- Piping tips (Nos. 1, 1.5, 2, 3, 14 star tip)
- Mini gold dragees
- Round No. 4 or No. 5 paintbrush
- Pink petal dust
- Fine black edible marker
- Toothpick
- White edible airbrush color
- Royal icing:

Light and medium electric pink (meringue consistency)

Egg yellow (honey consistency)

Lime green (meringue consistency)

White royal (meringue consistency)

1
Choose a basic cookie recipe on page 7, and make a batch of cookies using a butterfly cutter. Allow the cookies to cool completely before decorating. Trace the butterfly edges—leaving space for the antennae—using a yellow edible marker. Outline the butterfly using medium electric pink icing and No. 2 tip. Allow to dry completely.

2
Flood the butterfly using egg yellow icing and No. 3 tip. Allow to dry completely.

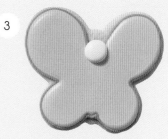

3
Pipe the head using lime green icing and No. 2 tip. Allow to dry completely.

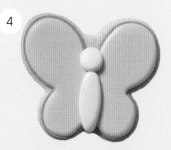

4
Outline and flood the body using the same green icing and tip. Allow to dry completely.

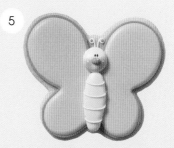

5
Pipe the antennae using lime green icing and No. 1.5 tip. Add gold dragees on the tips. Use a paintbrush to apply petal dust to the cheeks. Pipe an oval for the nose using light pink icing and No.1.5 tip. Draw eyes with a black edible marker. Dip a toothpick in white edible airbrush color and paint a dot on each cheek.

6
Start from the center of each wing and pipe swirl lines toward the edges using 2 shades of electric pink icing and No. 1.5 tip (see picture). While the icing is wet, add gold dragees to the tips. Pipe drops on the starting points of the swirl lines, one at a time, using the same icing and tip. Pipe a dot on top of each drop. While the icing is wet, add a gold dragee to each drop.

Flower Bouquet

I use both the wet-on-dry and wet-on-wet techniques for these beautiful bouquet cookies (see page 17). *NK*

SUPPLIES

- Mirror cookie cutter
- 6 piping bags
- Metal skewer or toothpick
- Royal icing (regular consistency):
  - Mint green
  - Leaf green
  - White
  - Pink
  - Fuchsia
  - Dark green

1. Choose a basic cookie recipe on page 7, and make a batch of cookies using a mirror cutter. Allow the cookies to cool completely before decorating. Prepare the piping bags by cutting a 1–2-mm hole for piping and a 3-mm hole for flooding.

2. Outline and flood the top part of the bouquet with mint green icing.

3. While the icing is wet, pipe green dots with leaf green icing. Use a metal skewer or toothpick to drag these dots into leaf shapes.

4. Pipe dots to position the flower buds using white, pink, and fuchsia icing. Allow to dry completely.

5. Using dark green icing, pipe lines from some of the flower buds to the bottom of the bouquet. Pipe a swirl rose on each bud using white, pink, and fuchsia icing (see page 16).

6. Pipe the bow on the bouquet using white icing. Allow to dry completely.

Monogram

These cookies are easily personalised for birthdays. I use royal icing transfers that have been piped and dried ahead of time. *NK*

SUPPLIES

- Scalloped oval cookie cutter
- 1 piping bag
- Yellow edible marker
- Patterned edible paper
- Scissors
- Royal icing (regular consistency):
  - White

1. Choose a basic cookie recipe on page 7, and make a batch of cookies using a scalloped oval cutter. Allow the cookies to cool completely before decorating. Prepare the piping bag by cutting a 3-mm hole for flooding.

2. Using a yellow edible marker, draw an oval onto patterned edible paper and cut it out.

3. Flood the cookie with white icing and place the oval paper gently on the cookie.

4. Make a transfer letter (see page 17) and use white icing to glue it on the cookie (do this very carefully, as transfers are delicate).

5. Pipe the monogram border and details with white icing. Allow to dry completely.

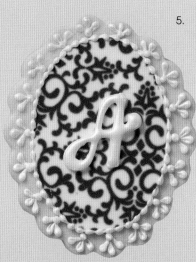

Purse

This is the perfect choice for anyone with a purse obsession! If the birthday girl has a favorite purse in her collection, adjust the colors to match and she'll get a real surprise when she sees the cookies. *MS*

SUPPLIES

- Purse cookie cutter
- Yellow edible marker
- 2 piping bags and couplers
- Piping tips (Nos. 1.5, 3)
  - Accent tweezers
- Black pearlized sugar pearls
- Silver pearlized sugar pearls
- Scribe tool or toothpick
  - Royal icing:

  White (honey consistency)

  Black (meringue consistency)

1. Choose a basic cookie recipe on page 7, and make a batch of cookies using a purse cutter. Allow the cookies to cool completely before decorating.

2. Trace the purse outline onto the cookie using a yellow edible marker.

3. Outline and flood the upper part of the purse using white icing and No. 3 tip. While the icing is wet, use tweezers to add a black sugar pearl for the button. Allow to dry for about 30 minutes.

4. Outline and flood the lower part of the purse using the same icing and tip. While the icing is wet, use tweezers to place a silver pearl on the lower right side of the purse. Immediately, add black pearls around it for flower petals. Allow to dry completely.

5. Outline the purse handle using black icing and No. 3 tip.

6. Pipe some short lines as seams on the purse using white icing and No. 1.5 tip. Allow to dry completely.

Shoe

Shoe cookies can be very fancy, or they can follow a simple and elegant design like this one. As with the purse cookie, you can match the colors on this design to the birthday girl's favorite pair of shoes. *NK*

SUPPLIES

- Shoe cookie cutter
- 3 piping bags
- Accent tweezers
- White sugar pearls
- Royal icing (regular consistency):
  - Ivory
  - White
  - Brown

1. Choose a basic cookie recipe on page 7, and make a batch of cookies using a shoe cutter. Allow the cookies to cool completely before decorating. Prepare the piping bags by cutting a 1–2-mm hole for piping and a 3-mm hole for flooding.

2. Outline and flood the main shoe section of the cookie with ivory icing. Allow to dry.

3. Flood the white part of the shoe with white icing. Allow to dry.

4. Pipe the bow using brown icing. Allow to dry completely.

5. Outline all the details again and use accent tweezers to add sugar pearls on the bow. Allow to dry completely.

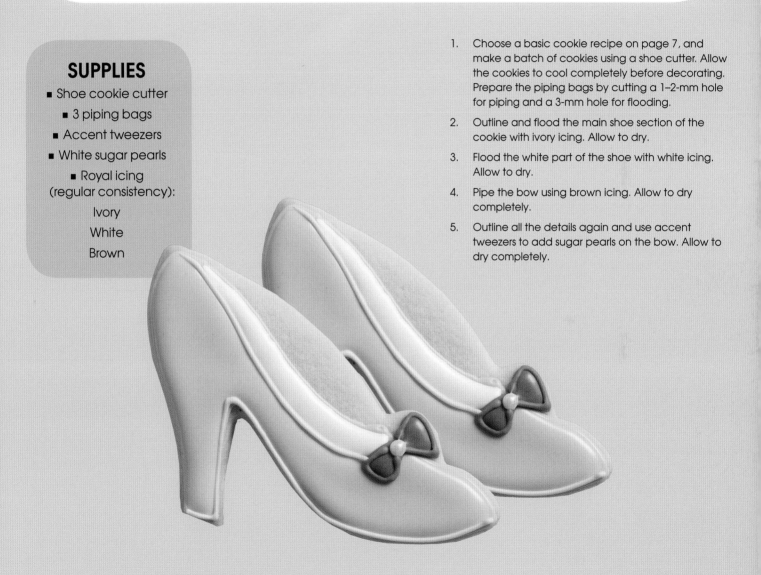

Camping

This colorful cookie will bring back happy memories of family vacations or trips away with friends. *NK*

Golf

Golf is a popular sport, so these cookies are a great go-to for birthday parties for friends and family. *NK*

SUPPLIES

- Scalloped square cookie cutter
- 9 piping bags
- Royal icing (regular consistency):

    White

    Black

    Light and dark blue

    Yellow

    Light and dark green

    Tan

    Red

1. Choose a basic cookie recipe on page 7, and make a batch of cookies using a scalloped square cutter. Allow the cookies to cool completely before decorating. Prepare the piping bags by cutting a 1–2-mm hole for piping and a 3-mm hole for flooding.

2. Outline and flood the cookie with white icing. Allow to dry completely.

3. Outline the tent with black icing. Flood the side of the tent and 2 front flaps with light blue icing. Flood the middle front section with dark blue icing. Pipe the sun beams with yellow icing.

4. Pipe the grass with light and dark green icing (see picture). Pipe the tent window with black icing.

5. Pipe the feet with tan icing. Pipe the tiny flowers with red and yellow icing.

6. Using dark green icing, pipe a border around the cookie by making teardrops. Allow to dry completely.

SUPPLIES

- Round cookie cutter
- 7 piping bags
- Royal icing (regular consistency):

    Leaf green

    Blue

    White

    Dark green

    Red

    Brown

    Black

1. Choose a basic cookie recipe on page 7, and make a batch of cookies using a round cutter. Allow the cookies to cool completely before decorating. Prepare the piping bags by cutting a 1–2-mm hole for piping and a 3-mm hole for flooding.

2. Outline and flood the lower part of the cookie with leaf green icing.

3. Outline and flood the upper part of the cookie with blue icing. While the icing is wet, use white icing to pipe spots on the upper part of the cookie to make clouds. Allow to dry completely.

4. Using dark green icing, pipe trees on both sides of the cookie. Pipe the flag using red and brown icing. Add the flag base using black icing.

5. Pipe the ball with white icing. Pipe little dots and birds with black icing.

6. Make a border around the green part of the cookie using dark green icing. Make a border around the upper part of the cookie using blue icing. Allow to dry completely.

Fishing

Anyone who loves fishing will be happy to receive these cookies on their birthday! This cookie is easy to make, but there are lots of small details that need to be accurate for the design to work. *NK*

SUPPLIES

- 3½-in (9-cm) circle cookie cutter
- 8 piping bags
- Metal skewer
- Royal icing (regular consistency):
  - Blue
  - White
  - Light and dark green
  - Yellow
  - Red
  - Black
  - Brown

1

Choose a basic cookie recipe on page 7, and make a batch of cookies using a circle cutter. Allow the cookies to cool completely before decorating. Prepare the piping bags by cutting a 1–2-mm hole for piping and a 3-mm hole for flooding. Outline and flood the bottom part of the cookie using blue icing. Create a wavy line along the top edge. While it is wet, outline and flood the top of the cookie with white icing.

2

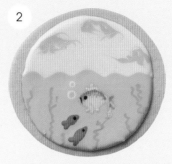

While the icing is wet, pipe spots in the sky with blue icing. Using a metal skewer, drag through the spots to make clouds. Using light and dark green icing, pipe wavy lines in the water to make plants. Pipe the fish with yellow icing. Add red icing on the back and tail, and drag it with the skewer to mix the colors. Pipe the eye and lips with black icing. Pipe 2 white icing dots with 2 blue icing dots inside them for bubbles. Pipe 2 more fish using red icing. Add black icing eyes.

3

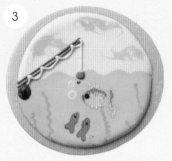

Using brown and dark green icing, pipe 2 parallel lines to make a fishing rod. Pipe the reel with brown and black icing. Pipe loops and a vertical line on the rod, using white icing, to make a fishing line. Pipe the fishing bobber with red and green icing.

4

Pipe the border with blue icing, creating dots around the cookie. Allow to dry completely.

Beer Mug

If you don't have a beer mug cookie cutter, draw a beer mug on paper, cut it out, and use it as a template on the dough. Use a sharp knife to cut the mug-shaped cookie. *NK*

SUPPLIES

- Beer mug cookie cutter (or paper, pencil, and knife)
- 3 piping bags
- Airbrush
- Orange edible airbrush color
- Brown edible airbrush color
- Pearl edible airbrush color
- Royal icing (regular consistency):

  Light orange

  White

  Gold

1. Choose a basic cookie recipe on page 7, and make a batch of cookies using a beer mug cutter (or paper template). Allow the cookies to cool completely before decorating. Prepare the piping bags by cutting a 1–2-mm hole for piping and a 3-mm hole for flooding.

2. Outline and flood the glass with light orange icing. While the icing is wet, pipe 2 vertical lines using white icing. Pipe white dots then pipe orange dots over some of them to make bubbles. Allow to dry completely.

3. Outline and flood the foam with white icing. Allow to dry completely.

4. Using an airbrush and orange edible airbrush color, spray down the left side of the cookie. Using brown edible airbrush color, make shadows and edges on the glass.

5. Pipe the handle of the glass with gold icing. Pipe bubbles onto the foam using white icing and allow some to drip down over the side of the glass. Allow to dry completely.

6. Using the airbrush and pearl edible airbrush color, spray over the whole cookie. Allow to dry completely.

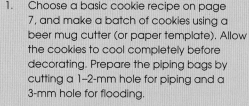

Candles

Make a wish on your special day with this friendly candle character. Make enough to represent the number of years being celebrated. *MS*

SUPPLIES

- Candle cookie cutter
- Yellow edible marker
- 5 piping bags and couplers
- Piping tips (Nos. 1.5, 2, 3)
- Accent tweezers
- Black edible pearls (⅛ in/4 mm)
- Round No. 4 or No. 5 paintbrush
- Pink petal dust
- Round no. 10/0 paintbrush
- White edible airbrush color
- Toothpick
- Fine black edible marker
- Royal icing:
  Lime green (honey consistency)
  Orange (honey consistency)
  Egg yellow (meringue consistency)
  Lime green (meringue consistency)
  White (meringue consistency)

1

Choose a basic cookie recipe on page 7, and make a batch of cookies using a candle cutter. Allow the cookies to cool completely before decorating. Use a yellow edible marker to divide the wax and flame. Outline and flood the wax using lime green icing (honey consistency) and No. 3 tip. While the icing is wet, add dots using orange icing and No. 2 tip. Allow to dry.

2

Outline and flood the flame using egg yellow icing and No. 2 tip. While the icing is wet, use accent tweezers to add black edible pearls as eyes. Allow to dry completely.

3

Using a paintbrush, apply petal dust to the cheeks and the curves of the flame. Paint highlights on the flame using a No. 10/0 paintbrush and white edible airbrush color. Pipe melted wax using lime green icing (meringue consistency) and No. 2 tip. Allow to dry.

4

Pipe the wick using white icing and No. 1.5 tip. Dip a toothpick in white edible airbrush color and paint a small dot on each cheek. Use a black edible marker to draw a smile. Allow to dry completely.

Cake with Candles

This topsy turvy cake with candles is inspired by the traditional cakes that are baked and decorated at home. There are no extra decorations—just frosting, sprinkles, and most importantly, the candles! *MS*

SUPPLIES

- Cake with sparklers cookie cutter
- Yellow edible marker
- 8 piping bags and couplers
- Piping tips (Nos. 1.5, 2, 3, 14)
- Scribe tool or toothpick
- Yellow edible glitter
- Multicolored nonpareils
- Royal icing:

Light brown (honey consistency)

Green (meringue consistency)

Orange (meringue consistency)

Blue (meringue consistency)

White (honey consistency)

Yellow (meringue consistency)

White (meringue consistency)

White (buttercream consistency)

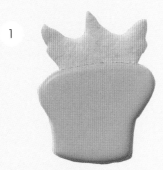

1 Choose a basic cookie recipe on page 7, and make a batch of cookies using a cake with sparklers cutter. Allow the cookies to cool completely before decorating. Use a yellow edible marker to divide the cake and candles. Outline and flood the cake using light brown icing and No. 3 tip. Allow to dry.

2 Pipe the candles using green, orange, and blue icing and No. 1.5 tip. Pipe slanted lines onto the candles using white icing (honey consistency) and No. 1.5 tip. Allow to dry.

3 Pipe the flames as drops using yellow icing and No. 1.5 tip. While the icing is wet, pipe a dot inside each flame using orange icing and No. 1.5 tip. Use a scribe tool or toothpick to drag the dot toward the end of the flame. While the icing is wet, add yellow edible glitter.

4 Outline and flood the frosting with white icing (honey consistency) and No. 3 tip. While the icing is wet, add nonpareils. Pipe and drag dots on the center using white icing (meringue consistency) and No. 2 tip. Pipe a line on the base using white icing (buttercream consistency) and No. 14 tip. Add nonpareils.

HOLIDAY PARTIES

Boy

For these cookies I use an upside-down snowman cookie cutter. *NK*

SUPPLIES

- Snowman cookie cutter
- 4 piping bags
- Metal skewer or toothpick
- Paintbrush
- Gold food color
- Flamingo blossom dust
- Royal icing (regular consistency):

  Tan

  Black

  Red

  White

1. Choose a basic cookie recipe on page 7, and make a batch of cookies using a snowman cutter. Allow the cookies to cool completely before decorating. Prepare the piping bags by cutting a 1–2-mm hole for piping and a 3-mm hole for flooding.
2. Outline and flood the head using tan icing. While the icing is wet, use a metal skewer or toothpick and black icing to draw the eyes, mouth, and brows. Allow to dry completely.
3. Pipe the nose, lips, ears, and neck using tan icing.
4. Outline and flood the hat, jacket, and pants using red icing. Allow to dry completely.
5. Pipe the sleeves using white icing. While the icing is wet, draw the folds on the sleeves using the skewer and black icing. Pipe the hands with tan icing.
6. Using black icing, pipe the hair, hat tassel, shoes, and jacket details. While the icing is wet, pipe small white dots on the shoes. Allow to dry completely.
7. Using a paintbrush and gold food color, draw the patterns on the jacket, pants, and hat. Use the paintbrush and flamingo blossom dust to paint the cheeks.

Girl

If you're hosting a Chinese New Year Party, you could make a batch of the boy cookies and a batch of the girl cookies. *NK*

SUPPLIES

- Snowman cookie cutter
- 5 piping bags
- Metal skewer or toothpick
- Paintbrush
- Gold food color
- Flamingo blossom dust
- Royal icing (regular consistency):

  Tan

  Black

  Red

  White

  Yellow

1. Choose a basic cookie recipe on page 7, and make a batch of cookies using a snowman cutter. Allow the cookies to cool completely before decorating. Prepare the piping bags by cutting a 1–2-mm hole for piping and a 3-mm hole for flooding.
2. Outline and flood the head using tan icing. While the icing is wet, use a metal skewer or toothpick and black icing to draw the eyes, mouth, and brows. Allow to dry completely.
3. Outline and flood the dress using red icing. Pipe the lips with red icing.
4. Pipe the hair using black icing. Use tan icing to pipe the ears, nose, neck, arms, and legs. Allow to dry completely.
5. Pipe the shoes, collar, and hairlines using black icing. While the icing is wet, pipe white dots on the shoes.
6. Pipe the lace (loops and dots) on the bottom of the dress using yellow icing. Pipe red lines on the hair to make ribbons.
7. Using a paintbrush and gold food color, paint little patterns on the dress (see picture). Draw the cheeks using the paintbrush and flamingo blossom dust. Allow to dry completely.

Dragon

The dragon is the most recognizable symbol of Chinese New Year, and the bold red color will make it stand out on your table. *NK*

SUPPLIES

- Dragon cookie cutter
- 5 piping bags
- Metal skewer or toothpick
- Gold food color
- Paintbrush
- Royal icing (regular consistency):

  Red

  Yellow

  Brown

  Black

  White

1. Choose a basic cookie recipe on page 7, and make a batch of cookies using a dragon cutter. Allow the cookies to cool completely before decorating. Prepare the piping bags by cutting a 1–2-mm hole for piping and a 3-mm hole for flooding.

2. Outline and flood the body with red icing. While the icing is wet, pipe the front part of the body with yellow icing. Using a metal skewer or toothpick, drag it through the red and yellow icing to blend the colors. Repeat the same process on the wing tips using brown icing.

3. While the icing is wet, pipe a black and white dot to make an eye. Use a skewer to drag through the black part of the eye. Allow to dry completely.

4. Use red icing to pipe the paws. Outline the wing and pipe the webs on the wings using red icing.

5. Pipe the claws, mouth, and small details and lines on the tail and neck using red icing. Allow to dry completely.

6. Using gold food color and a paintbrush, make strokes on the wings and paint all the small details. Allow to dry completely.

Firecracker

Firecrackers are a Chinese tradition that are used all over the world to celebrate Chinese New Year. *MS*

SUPPLIES

- Shooting star cookie cutter
- 5 piping bags and couplers
- Piping tips (Nos. 1.5, 2, 3, 301)
- Mini square cookie cutter
- Silver edible marker
- Toothpick
- Yellow sanding sugar
- Royal icing:

  Red (meringue consistency)

  Yellow (meringue consistency)

  Yellow (10-second consistency)

  Orange (10-second consistency)

  Black (meringue consistency)

1. Choose a basic cookie recipe on page 7, and make a batch of cookies using a shooting star cutter. Before baking, cut the tail and sides to make a cylinder shape. Allow the cookies to cool completely before decorating.

2. Outline and flood the cylinder using red icing and No. 3 tip. Allow to dry completely.

3. Outline the explosion using yellow icing (meringue consistency) and No. 2 tip. Allow to dry.

4. Pipe 2 lines in the cylinder using yellow icing (meringue consistency) and No. 301 tip.

5. Use a mini square cutter and silver edible marker to trace the central shape. Pipe the lines using the same icing and No. 1.5 tip. Allow to dry.

6. Fill the explosion with yellow icing (10-second consistency) and No. 3 tip. While the icing is wet, pipe a dot in the middle, using orange icing and No. 3 tip. Pipe a smaller dot in the center. Use a toothpick to drag the dot from the center to each peak. Allow to dry.

7. Pipe a line for a wick using black icing and No. 1.5 tip.

8. Pipe a line around the explosion using yellow icing (meringue consistency) and No. 2 tip. While the icing is wet, pour yellow sanding sugar on the border. Allow to dry.

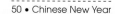

Lantern

These cute, little Chinese lanterns can be made with other cookies for a New Year party. *MS*

SUPPLIES

- Chinese lantern cookie cutter
- 3 piping bags and couplers
- Piping tips (Nos. 1.5, 2, 3)
- Airbrush
- Brown edible airbrush color
- Royal icing:

Red (honey consistency)

Egg yellow (meringue consistency)

Green (meringue consistency)

1

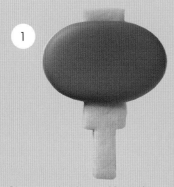

Choose a basic cookie recipe on page 7, and make a batch of cookies using a Chinese lantern cutter. Allow the cookies to cool completely before decorating. Outline and flood the lantern using red icing and No. 3 tip. Allow to dry completely.

2

Using an airbrush and brown edible airbrush color, airbrush the lantern edges. Allow to dry completely.

3

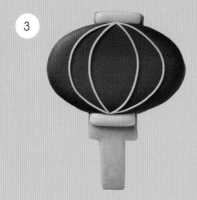

Pipe yellow rectangle areas on the top and bottom of the lantern using egg yellow icing and No. 2 tip. Change the tip to No. 1.5 and pipe the curved yellow lines on the lantern. Allow to dry completely.

4

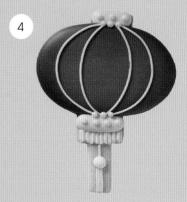

Using the same icing and tip, pipe decorative dots on the yellow details (see picture). Pipe a layer of tassels with a longer line in the center. Pipe a green dot down the longer yellow line using green icing and No. 1.5 tip. Pipe 3 straight yellow lines under the green dot. Finally, pipe a second layer of tassels in between the first ones.

Sweetheart

These classic Valentine cookies are just irresistible. Turn them into a special gift by wrapping each cookie in clear cellophane and tying the ends with ribbon. You can also make a cute gift box full of these cookies. 𝓜𝓢

SUPPLIES

- Candy cookie cutter (or 1½-in/4-cm and 1¼-in/3-cm heart-shaped cookie cutters)
- Yellow edible marker
- 2 piping bags and couplers
- Piping tips (Nos. 1.5, 2)
- Scribe tool or toothpick
- Royal icing (meringue consistency):
  Super red
  White

1. Choose a basic cookie recipe on page 7, and make a batch of cookies using a candy cutter. Allow the cookies to cool completely before decorating.

2. Trace the hearts using a yellow edible marker and the provided template (see pages 134–139).

3. Outline and flood the central heart using super red icing and No. 2 tip. Allow to dry.

4. Outline and flood the cookie sides using white icing and No. 1.5 tip. Allow to dry.

5. Pipe swirls and dots around the edge of the central heart using the same red icing and No. 1.5 tip (see picture).

6. Pipe swirls and dots on the sides of the cookie using white icing and No. 1.5 tip (see picture).

Red Heart

This simple and elegant cookie heart is the perfect choice for Valentine's Day. Here, it is decorated in red, but it also looks lovely in white or pink. *MS*

SUPPLIES

- 2¾- x 3-in (7- x 8-cm) heart cookie cutter
- 3 piping bags and couplers
- Piping tips (Nos. 1.5, 3)
- Royal icing:

Super red (honey consistency)

Pastel pink (buttercream consistency)

Lime green (buttercream consistency)

1. Choose a basic cookie recipe on page 7, and make a batch of cookies using a heart cutter. Allow the cookies to cool completely before decorating.

2. Outline and flood the cookie using super red icing and No. 3 tip. Allow to dry.

3. Outline the crossed lines on the cookie surface using the same red icing and No. 1.5 tip (see picture). Pipe red dots on each line intersection and allow to dry.

4. Pipe small swirl roses (see page 17) using pink icing and No. 1.5 tip. Pipe 2 leaves around every rose using lime green icing and No. 1.5 tip. Allow to dry completely.

TIPS & TRICKS

If you don't feel confident piping straight lines, practice on parchment paper before decorating the cookie.

Lips

These cookie lips are simple to make. If you like, you can use a very thin paintbrush to draw some lines onto the lips, using a lighter shade of food coloring diluted in water. This will make it look as if your cookie is sending a kiss. 𝓜𝓢

Lovebirds

These lovebirds will be perfect not only for Valentine's Day, but also for weddings and anniversaries. 𝓜𝓢

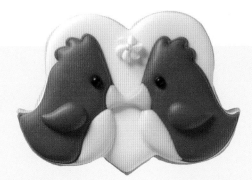

SUPPLIES

- Lips cookie cutter
- Spatula
- Brown edible marker
- 3 piping bags and couplers
- Piping tips (Nos. 1.5, 2)
- Scribe tool or toothpick
- Royal icing (honey consistency):
  Black
  Electric pink
  White

1. Choose a basic cookie recipe on page 7, and make a batch of cookies using a lips cutter. Allow the cookies to cool completely before decorating.
2. Use a spatula to spread a thin layer of black icing in the center of the cookie and allow to dry.
3. Trace the lips using a brown edible marker.
4. Outline and flood the upper lip using electric pink icing and No. 2 tip.
5. While the icing is wet, pipe the shine on the upper left side of the lip using white icing and No. 1.5 tip. Allow to dry.
6. Pipe and flood the lower lip using the same pink icing and tip. While the icing is wet, pipe the shine on the lower lip using the same white icing and tip. Allow to dry completely.

TIPS & TRICKS

You can use the scribe tool to drag the white icing lines on the lips.

SUPPLIES

- Lovebirds cookie cutter
- Royal icing flower transfers
- 5 piping bags and couplers
- Piping tips (Nos. 1.5, 2, 3)
- Silver edible marker
- Accent tweezers
- Edible black pearls
- Royal icing:
  White (honey consistency)
  Red (meringue consistency)
  Ivory (meringue consistency)
  Yellow (meringue consistency)

1. Choose a basic cookie recipe on page 7, and make a batch of cookies using a lovebirds cutter. Allow the cookies to cool completely before decorating.
2. Make the icing flower transfers in advance (see page 17).
3. Outline and flood the cookie using white icing and No. 3 tip. Allow to dry completely.
4. Trace the birds using a silver edible marker and the provided template (see pages 134–141).
5. Outline the birds using red, ivory, and yellow icing and No. 1.5 tip (see picture).
6. Flood the red area using the same icing and No. 2 tip. While the icing is wet, use tweezers to add edible black pearls as eyes.
7. Fill the ivory area using the same icing and No. 1.5 tip. Fill the beak using yellow icing and No. 1.5 tip. Allow to dry.
8. Pipe the wings using red icing and No. 1.5 tip. Glue a flower on top of the heart. Allow to dry.

Leprechaun

This cheerful leprechaun's rosy grin is an essential part of any St. Patrick's Day celebration. The beard looks tricky but it's actually fairly quick and easy to create with a little practice. *MS*

SUPPLIES

- Leprechaun cookie cutter
  - Brown edible marker
  - 5 piping bags and couplers
  - Piping tips (Nos. 1.5, 2, 3, 14 star tip)
  - Accent tweezers
- Colored heart sprinkles
- Round No. 4 or No. 5 paintbrush
  - Pink petal dust
  - Toothpick
- White edible airbrush color
- Fine black edible marker
  - Royal icing:

Flesh (honey consistency)

Lime green (honey consistency)

Black (meringue consistency)

Orange (buttercream consistency)

Egg yellow (meringue consistency)

1. Choose a basic cookie recipe on page 7, and make a batch of cookies using a leprechaun cutter. Allow the cookies to cool completely before decorating. Trace the leprechaun using a brown edible marker and the provided template (see pages 134–139). Outline and flood the face using flesh icing and No. 3 tip. Allow to dry.

2. Outline and flood the hat using lime green icing and No. 3 tip. While the icing is wet, use accent tweezers to add 4 heart sprinkles in different colors to create a shamrock. Allow to dry. Outline and flood the brim of the hat and allow to dry.

3. Pipe the black ribbon across the base of the hat using black icing and No. 2 tip. Pipe the eyebrows using orange icing and No. 14 tip. Using the same icing and tip, decorate the beard by piping small spirals, starting from one side and working across to the other side. Pipe the nose using flesh icing and No. 1.5 tip.

4. Pipe the buckle on the hat ribbon using yellow icing and No. 2 tip. Pipe a zigzag line onto the ribbon using black icing and No. 1.5 tip. Decorate the brim by piping green swirls and dots, using green icing and No. 1.5 tip. Using a paintbrush, apply pink petal dust to the cheeks. Pipe the ears using flesh icing and No. 1.5 tip.

5. Add green dots to the shamrock using lime green icing and No. 1.5 tip. Dip a toothpick in white edible airbrush color and paint a small dot on each cheek. Draw the eyes and smile with a black edible marker.

Pot of Gold

Who wouldn't like to find a pot of gold at the end of the rainbow? With these fun cookies and the luck of the Irish...who knows. *MS*

SUPPLIES

- Pot of gold cookie cutter
- Yellow edible marker
- 7 piping bags and couplers
- Piping tips (Nos. 1.5, 2, 3)
- Gold sanding sugar
- Silver edible marker
- Small heart cookie cutter
- Accent tweezers
- Mini gold dragees
- Round No. 4 or No. 5 paintbrush
- Green petal dust
- Royal icing:

Lime green (meringue consistency)

Leaf green (honey consistency)

Yellow (meringue consistency)

White (meringue consistency)

Orange (meringue consistency)

Electric pink (meringue consistency)

Blue (meringue consistency)

1. Choose a basic cookie recipe on page 7, and make a batch of cookies using a pot of gold cutter. Allow the cookies to cool completely before decorating.

2. Trace the pot of gold divisions using a yellow edible marker.

3. Outline and flood the pot using lime green icing and No. 3 tip. Allow to dry.

4. Outline and flood the legs of the pot using leaf green icing and No. 1.5 tip. With the same icing and tip, outline and flood the top of the pot. Allow to dry.

5. Outline and flood the gold using yellow icing and No. 2 tip. While the icing is wet, pour gold sanding sugar on it. Allow to dry.

6. Use a silver edible marker and a small heart-shaped cookie cutter to trace the shamrock.

7. Outline and flood a highlight on the left side of the pot using white icing and No. 1.5 tip.

8. Pipe the upper leaf of the shamrock, following the heart shape, using orange icing and No. 1.5 tip. Allow to dry for about 30 minutes before piping the second leaf, using pink icing and No. 1.5 tip. Wait another 30 minutes and pipe the last leaf using blue icing and No. 1.5 tip. Allow to dry enough, then pipe the stem using yellow icing and No. 1.5 tip.

9. Pipe a dot in the center of the clover using the same yellow icing and tip. While the icing is wet, use tweezers to add 1 mini gold dragee on the dot.

10. Using the paintbrush, apply green petal dust to make the shadows on the pot of gold (see picture).

Rainbow

The royal icing used to make this beautiful rainbow cookie will help you decorate it quickly. Make sure you mix plenty of each color icing, as this design uses more than others. *MS*

SUPPLIES

- Rainbow cookie cutter (approx. 3½ x 2¾ in/ 9 x 7 cm)
- 7 piping bags and couplers
- Piping tips (No. 10 round tip)
- White edible glitter
- Royal icing (buttercream consistency):
    Pastel violet
    Pastel blue
    Pastel green
    Pastel yellow
    Pastel orange
    Pastel pink
    White

1. Choose a basic cookie recipe on page 7, and make a batch of cookies using a rainbow cutter. Allow the cookies to cool completely before decorating.

2. This design doesn't need every color division traced, as the round tip will help you to pipe each line. But, if you feel more confident having a guide to keep the lines at the same width, feel free to do so.

3. Using violet icing and No. 10 tip, tilt the piping bag at 45 degrees. Very gently pipe the inner line of the rainbow. Start piping on the left side of the cookie and work toward the right side. With the help of your free hand, rotate the cookie while piping to achieve a neat, curved line. This icing consistency dries fast so you don't need to let it dry completely before piping the next line.

4. Pipe the second line around the first using the same technique. Use blue icing and the same tip.

5. Pipe the rest of the lines using the same technique and tip. Pipe each line close to the previous one to avoid gaps, and apply the same pressure on the icing bag to get the same line width.

6. Finish the cookie by piping dots of white icing for clouds at either end of the rainbow. Dust with white edible glitter and allow to dry.

Shamrock

To make these shamrock leaves more fun, I add ladybugs to them. *NK*

SUPPLIES

- Shamrock cookie cutter
- 4 piping bags
- Royal icing (regular consistency):
    Green leaf
    Light green
    Red
    Black

1. Choose a basic cookie recipe on page 7, and make a batch of cookies using a shamrock cutter. Allow the cookies to cool completely before decorating. Prepare the piping bags by cutting a 1–2-mm hole for piping and a 3-mm hole for flooding.

2. Outline and flood the cookie in green leaf icing. While the icing is wet, pipe the hearts in every leaf using light green icing. Allow to dry completely.

3. Pipe the body of the ladybug with red icing. While the icing is wet, pipe the black dots and the head using black icing. Allow to dry completely.

Egg

Everyone eats too many chocolate eggs at Easter time, so these pretty little cookies will make a nice change for an Easter treat. *MS*

SUPPLIES

- Egg cookie cutter
- 7 piping bags and couplers
- Piping tips (Nos. 1.5, 2, 3)
- Silver edible marker
- Scribe tool or toothpick
- Royal icing (pastel colors):

  White (honey consistency)

  Pink (meringue consistency)

  Green (meringue consistency)

  Yellow (meringue consistency)

  Orange (meringue consistency)

  Violet (meringue consistency)

  Teal (meringue consistency)

1. Choose a basic cookie recipe on page 7, and make a batch of cookies using an egg cutter. Allow the cookies to cool completely before decorating.

2. Outline and flood the egg using white icing and No. 3 tip. Allow to dry completely.

3. Using the provided template (see pages 134–139), trace the main decorative lines onto the background with a silver edible marker.

4. Outline and flood the wide pink wavy line on the upper side of the egg using pink icing and No. 2 tip. Outline and flood the wide green wavy line on the lower side of the egg using green icing and No. 2 tip. It is not necessary to let it dry completely—you can keep decorating the rest of the cookie, trying not to touch the previous decorations.

5. To make the 3 flowers, pipe 1 big dot in the center of the egg using yellow icing and No. 1.5 tip. Pipe 2 smaller dots at each side using the same icing and tip. Allow to dry for about 10 minutes.

6. Make the petals by piping 3 equidistant dots using pink icing and No. 1.5 tip. Do the same with the smaller flowers using pink and violet icing and No. 1.5 tip. Allow to dry for about 10 minutes before piping 3 more dots in the free spaces. Pipe the leaves using green icing and No. 1.5 tip.

7. Using the picture as a guide, pipe the remaining lines and dots, combining the colors as you desire and using No. 1.5 tip. Be careful not to damage the previous lines and dots. You don't need to use No. 1.5 tips for all the decorations—you can use No. 1 tips, tipless piping bags, or the tool of your preference.

Chick

This cute, newborn chick will rock your party. This is a great design to get the kids to help out with, especially if you're hosting an Easter children's party or egg hunt. *MS*

SUPPLIES

- Egg cookie cutter
- Yellow edible marker
- 9 piping bags and couplers
- Piping tips (Nos. 1.5, 2)
- White sanding sugar
- Round No. 4 or No. 5 paintbrush
  - Pink petal dust
  - Toothpick
- White edible airbrush color
- Fine black edible marker
  - Royal icing:

White (meringue and 10-second consistency)

Lime green (10-second consistency)

Yellow (10-second consistency)

Purple (10-second consistency)

Blue (10-second consistency)

Pink (10-second consistency)

Egg yellow (honey consistency)

Orange (meringue consistency)

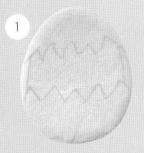

1 Choose a basic cookie recipe on page 7, and make a batch of cookies using an egg cutter. Allow the cookies to cool completely before decorating. Trace the broken shell using a yellow edible marker and the provided template (see pages 134–139).

2 Outline the broken shell using white icing (meringue consistency) and No. 1.5 tip. Allow to dry.

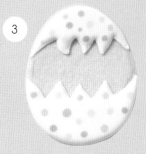

3 Flood the upper broken egg using white icing (10-second consistency) and No. 2 tip. While the icing is wet, pipe dots using all the 10-second consistency icing colors and No. 1.5 tip. Do the same with the lower broken egg and allow to dry.

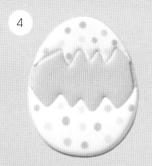

4 Fill the chick using yellow icing (honey consistency) and No. 2 tip. Allow to dry completely.

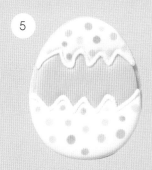

5 Pipe an outline onto the zigzag lines of the shell using white icing (meringue consistency) and No. 2 tip. While the icing is wet, pour sanding sugar over it. Allow to dry completely.

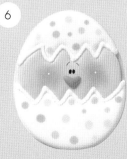

6 Use a paintbrush to apply pink petal dust to the cheeks. Make the beak by piping a triangular shape using orange icing and No. 1.5 tip. Dip a toothpick in white edible airbrush color and paint a small dot on each cheek. Draw eyes and eyebrows using a fine black edible marker.

Basket

I usually use an egg cookie cutter for basket cookies. The No. 47 tip gives a basket weave effect, which makes it far easier than it looks to create this eye-catching Easter design. *NK*

SUPPLIES

- Egg cookie cutter
- 8 piping bags
- Piping tips (Nos. 47, 65s)
- Airbrush
- Brown edible airbrush color
- Fine black edible marker
- Royal icing (regular consistency):

   Brown

   Yellow

   Blue

   Fuchsia

   Medium and dark green

   Red

   White

1. Choose a basic cookie recipe on page 7, and make a batch of cookies using an egg cutter. Allow the cookies to cool completely before decorating. For piping bags without tips, cut a 1–2-mm hole for piping and a 3-mm hole for flooding.

2. Outline the basket using brown icing. Make a basket weave effect by piping short horizontal lines across vertical lines using brown icing and No. 47 tip.

3. Pipe eggs on top of the basket using yellow, blue, and fuchsia icing.

4. Pipe the border around the main part of the basket. Pipe the short line around the basket handle.

5. Pipe medium green and dark green leaves with No. 65s tip. Pipe the tiny stems and flowers using red and white icing.

6. Using an airbrush and brown edible airbrush color, spray around the basket to make a shadow.

7. Use a black edible marker to draw tiny dots on every egg. Allow to dry completely.

Bunny Tail

Everyone loves cute Easter bunnies. These bunny tail cookies will make a lovely addition to a gift basket or the centerpiece for a party table. *NK*

SUPPLIES

- Egg cookie cutter
- 7 piping bags
- White sprinkles
- Royal icing (regular consistency):
  Brown
  White
  Medium and dark green
  Pink
  Fuchsia
  Yellow

1

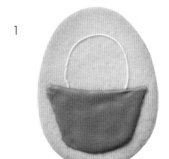

Choose a basic cookie recipe on page 7, and make a batch of cookies using an egg cutter. Allow the cookies to cool completely before decorating. Prepare the piping bags by cutting a 1–2-mm hole for piping and a 3-mm hole for flooding. Outline and flood the basket with brown icing. Outline the body with white icing.

2

Flood the bunny's body with white icing. Pipe the vertical lines on the basket using brown icing. Pipe short horizontal lines crossing the vertical lines to create a basket weave effect. Create bead borders with brown icing on the top and bottom of the basket.

3

Pipe the grass using medium green and dark green icing. Pipe the bunny paws using white icing. While the icing is wet, pipe the pink pads of the paws. Add toes with white icing and outline the pink part of the paws.

4

Pipe the bunny tail with white icing. While it is wet, put white sprinkles on the tail. Pipe tiny flowers on the basket, using pink, fuchsia, and yellow icing. Pipe white petals. Allow to dry completely.

Bunny Face

This bunny face is one of my daughter's favorite cookies. It reminds me of a popular cartoon from my childhood, and makes the perfect, classic Easter cookie. *NK*

SUPPLIES

- Bunny face cookie cutter
- 4 piping bags
- Metal skewer or toothpick
- Royal icing (regular consistency):
  White
  Pink
  Black
  Light blue

1 Choose a basic cookie recipe on page 7, and make a batch of cookies using a bunny face cutter. Allow the cookies to cool completely before decorating. Prepare the piping bags by cutting a 1–2-mm hole for piping and a 3-mm hole for flooding. Outline and flood the bunny with white icing.

2 While the icing is wet, add pink icing for the ears. Allow to dry. Pipe the eyes using black icing. Pipe the cheeks using white icing and use a metal skewer or toothpick to apply black icing dots for whiskers.

3 Pipe the nose and mouth using pink icing. Pipe the bow under the face with light blue icing and add white icing dots.

4 Outline the face and ears with white icing. Pipe the eyebrows with white icing. Allow to dry completely.

Lime Slice

A Cinco de Mayo party wouldn't be complete without lime slices. You will need to work fast to create the wet-on-wet effect before the icing forms a crust. *MS*

SUPPLIES

- 3½-in (9-cm) round cookie cutter
- 4 piping bags and couplers
- Piping tips (Nos. 1.5, 2, 3, 5)
- Toothpick
- White sanding sugar
- Paintbrush
- Royal icing:

Leaf green (meringue consistency)

White (meringue consistency)

Lime green (10-second consistency)

White (10-second consistency)

1. Choose a basic cookie recipe on page 7, and make a batch of cookies using a round cutter. Before baking, use a knife to cut the circles in half to create lime shapes. Allow the cookies to cool completely before decorating.

2. Outline the border using leaf green icing and No. 5 tip. Pipe a line on the edge of the cookie using white icing and No. 2 tip.

3. Pipe a second line next to the leaf green line using lime green icing and No. 2 tip. Immediately pipe a wider line next to the previous one using white icing and No. 2 tip. While the icing is wet, flood the rest of the cookie using lime green icing and No. 3 tip.

4. Using a toothpick, drag the icing from the wide white line toward the center of the circle. Repeat to create 4 segment outlines in total. Clean the tip of the toothpick before dragging each new line to prevent color contamination.

5. While the icing is wet, use white icing and No. 1.5 tip to pipe a few white drops for seeds and a dot in the lime center. Gently shake the cookie to get a smooth surface. Allow to dry completely.

6. Pipe a line along the straight border using white icing and No. 2 tip. While the icing is wet, pour over sanding sugar to represent salt. Allow to dry. Remove excess sugar with a paintbrush.

Piñata

Piñatas are one of the most widely gifted Cinco de Mayo party favors. This cookie is very easy to make. *MS*

SUPPLIES

- Piñata cookie cutter
- Brown edible marker
- 5 piping bags and couplers
- Piping tip (No. 2)
- Accent tweezers
- Royal icing eye (see page 17)
- Scribe tool or toothpick
- Royal icing (buttercream consistency):

Yellow

Orange

Lime green

Electric pink

Blue

1. Choose a basic cookie recipe on page 7, and make a batch of cookies using a piñata or donkey cutter. Allow the cookies to cool completely before decorating.

2. Use a brown edible marker to divide the ear, snout, and tail areas. Trace horizontal guidelines onto the rest of the cookie. Each line must be 5 mm (½ cm) apart.

3. Begin with the head. Using yellow icing and No. 2 tip, pipe the first horizontal line as a zigzag under the ear, tilting the piping bag at 45 degrees. Squeeze with an even pressure, trying to keep the zigzag in between the guidelines to avoid wider lines.

4. Pipe the first 4 lines using the picture as a guide to follow the color order. It is not necessary to leave each line to dry before piping the next one. While the icing is wet, use accent tweezers to add the royal icing eye.

5. Once all the horizontal lines are complete, pipe the lines on the snout and ear.

6. Pipe the upper tail using orange royal icing. Pipe the rest of the tail with a zigzag line in pink royal icing.

Taco

Everyone loves tacos, and these cute cookies look really authentic. *NK*

SUPPLIES

- Circle cookie cutter
- Knife
- 5 piping bags
- Royal icing (regular consistency):
  Gold
  Brown
  Green
  Red
  Yellow

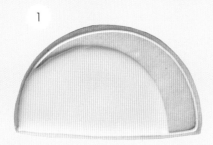

1

Choose a basic cookie recipe on page 7, and make a batch of cookies using a circle cutter. Before baking, use a knife to cut the circles in half to create taco shapes. Allow the cookies to cool completely before decorating. Prepare the piping bags by cutting a 1–2-mm hole for piping and a 3-mm hole for flooding. Outline the cookie with gold icing. Outline and flood the bigger section with gold icing.

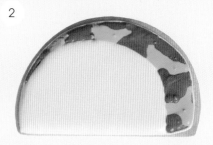

2

Pipe brown, green, and red spots on the thinner part of the taco.

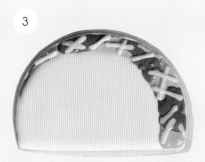

3

Using yellow icing, pipe short lines on the thinner part of the taco to resemble shredded cheese.

4

Outline the gold part of the taco with gold icing. Allow to dry completely.

Cactus

This is one of my simplest cookies and also one of the most fun to make. I hope it helps to make your celebration memorable. *MS*

SUPPLIES

- Cactus cookie cutter
- 5 piping bags and couplers
- Piping tips (Nos. 1.5, 2, 3, 5)
- Round No. 10/0 paintbrush
- White edible airbrush color
- Royal icing:

Leaf green (meringue consistency)

Leaf green (10-second consistency)

Lime green (10-second consistency)

Electric pink (meringue consistency)

Black (meringue consistency)

1 Choose a basic cookie recipe on page 7, and make a batch of cookies using a cactus cutter. Allow the cookies to cool completely before decorating. Outline the cactus using leaf green icing (meringue consistency) and No. 2 tip. Allow to dry completely.

2 Flood the cactus using leaf green icing (10-second consistency) and No. 2 tip. While the icing is wet, pipe lime green lines to simulate the cactus texture. Some of the lines should be wavy. Allow to dry completely.

3 Pipe an oval shape for a nose using electric pink icing and No. 1.5 tip. Using the same icing, change to No. 3 tip and pipe the petals on top of each arm. Squeeze hard to make the base wider and gradually release.

4 Pipe the eyes using black icing and No. 1.5 tip. Pipe the mustache, squeezing one side at a time. Allow to dry for 20 minutes before piping the second side. Paint the cactus spines using a paintbrush and white edible airbrush color (see picture).

Witch

This pretty witch will be the perfect Halloween treat. You can experiment with different colors to see which work best for your theme. *MS*

SUPPLIES

- Witch cookie cutter
- Yellow edible marker
- 6 piping bags and couplers
- Piping tips (Nos. 1.5, 2, 3)
- Accent tweezers
- Edible black pearls (⅛ in/4 mm)
- Yellow moon, blue star, and yellow star sprinkles
- Round No. 4 or No. 5 paintbrush
- Pink petal dust
- Scribe tool or toothpick
- White edible airbrush color
- Royal icing:

Flesh (meringue consistency)

Egg yellow (meringue consistency)

Light and medium purple (honey consistency)

Orange (honey consistency)

Brown (meringue consistency)

1 Choose a basic cookie recipe on page 7, and make a batch of cookies using a witch cutter. Allow the cookies to cool completely before decorating. Use a yellow edible marker to draw the outline of the witch. Outline and flood the face using flesh icing and No. 2 tip. Add edible black pearls as eyes. Outline and flood the broom using yellow icing and No. 2 tip.

2 Outline and flood the hat using light purple icing and No. 2 tip. Next, outline and flood the dress using medium purple icing and No. 2 tip. While the icing is wet, add a moon and 2 blue star sprinkles on the skirt (see picture). Allow to dry.

3 Pipe the sleeves with the same purple icing and No. 1.5 tip. Carefully fill the chest with flesh icing and No. 1.5 tip. Allow to dry.

4 Outline and flood the hair using orange icing and No. 2 tip. Pipe the hands using flesh icing and No. 1.5 tip. Pipe the hat and dress belts using orange icing and No. 3 tip. While the icing is wet, add a yellow star sprinkle onto each belt.

5 Pipe the broomstick using brown icing and No. 1.5 tip.

6 Pipe outlines onto the hat, hair, dress, and broom using matching icing colors and No. 1.5 tip. Pipe orange and yellow dots onto the star sprinkles. If needed, add a little powdered sugar to make the icing thicker. Use a paintbrush to apply pink petal dust to the cheeks. Dip a scribe tool or toothpick in white edible airbrush color and paint a small dot on each cheek.

Spider

This little guy will look great on your Halloween party table. Combine this cookie with a cat, a bat, or other themed cookie to create a stunning centerpiece. *MS*

SUPPLIES

- Spiderweb cookie cutter
- 4 piping bags and couplers
- Piping tips (Nos. 1.5, 2, 3)
- Toothpick
- Royal icing eyes (see page 17)
- Royal icing:

Purple (meringue consistency)

White (10-second consistency)

Black (meringue consistency)

Orange (meringue consistency)

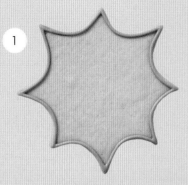

1 Choose a basic cookie recipe on page 7, and make a batch of cookies using a spiderweb cutter. Allow the cookies to cool completely before decorating. Outline the cookie using purple icing and No. 2 tip.

2 Flood the cookie using white icing and No. 3 tip. Immediately pipe a dot in the center of the cookie, then pipe concentric circles around the dot using purple icing and No. 1.5 tip. Starting from the center of the cookie, drag the dot toward each peak using a toothpick.

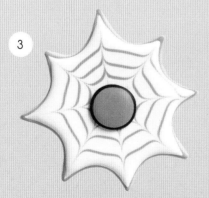

3 Pipe the outline of the spider using black icing and No. 2 tip. Allow to dry for about 30 minutes. Flood the spider using orange icing and No. 2 tip.

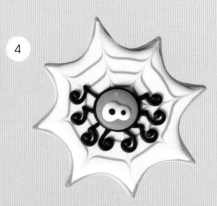

4 While the icing is wet, add royal icing eyes (see page 17). Allow to dry. Pipe the legs using the same black icing and No. 3 tip.

Ghost

When I was young, a simple bed sheet with holes was my favorite ghost disguise. This little character recreates that costume and will be perfect for trick-or-treaters. *MS*

SUPPLIES

- Ghost cookie cutter
- 5 piping bags and couplers
- Piping tips (Nos. 1.5, 2, 3)
- Accent tweezers
- Edible black pearls (1/8 in/4 mm)
- Black nonpareils
- Round No. 4 or No. 5 paintbrush
- Pink petal dust
- Toothpick
- White edible airbrush color
- Fine black edible marker
- Blue petal dust
- Royal icing:

Pastel blue (meringue consistency)

White (10-second consistency)

Royal blue (meringue consistency)

Flesh (meringue consistency)

Orange (meringue consistency)

1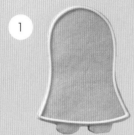

Choose a basic cookie recipe on page 7, and make a batch of cookies using a ghost cutter. Allow the cookies to cool completely before decorating. Outline the ghost using pastel blue icing and No. 3 tip. Allow to dry.

2

Flood the cookie using white icing and No. 3 tip. Use accent tweezers to add black edible pearls for eyes. Pipe the feet using royal blue icing and No. 1.5 tip. Allow to dry completely.

3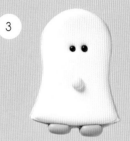

Using flesh icing and No. 2 tip, pipe a dot in the center of the ghost for hands.

4

Using the same icing and tip, pipe drop-shaped arms, trying to keep the wrists thinner. Make the pumpkin by piping a dot using orange icing and No. 1.5 tip. Immediately pipe an oval on either side of the dot. While the icing is wet, use the tweezers to add 2 nonpareils as pumpkin eyes. Allow to dry.

5

Using a paintbrush, apply pink petal dust to the cheeks. Dip a toothpick in white edible airbrush color and paint a small dot on each cheek. Draw eyebrows, a smile, and the pumpkin handle using a fine black edible marker. Use the paintbrush to gently apply blue petal dust on the sheet edges.

Frankenstein

The simple color combination of this cookie is very effective. You can hand these out as party favors, or add to the Halloween party table. *M$*

SUPPLIES

- Frankenstein cookie cutter
- Yellow edible marker
- 5 piping bags and couplers
- Piping tips (Nos. 1.5, 3, 5)
  - Accent tweezers
  - Edible black pearls (⅛ in/4 mm)
- Round No. 4 or No. 5 paintbrush
  - Pink petal dust
  - Toothpick
- White edible airbrush color
- Fine black edible marker
  - Silver luster dust
  - Edible alcohol
  - Royal icing:

Black (honey consistency)

Light green (meringue consistency)

Gray (meringue consistency)

Flesh (meringue consistency)

1. Choose a basic cookie recipe on page 7, and make a batch of cookies using a Frankenstein cutter. Allow the cookies to cool completely before decorating. Using a yellow edible marker, trace the wavy division between the face and hair. Outline and flood the hair using black icing and No. 1.5 tip. Allow to dry.

2. Outline and flood the face using light green icing and No. 3 tip. While the icing is wet, use accent tweezers to add edible black pearls as eyes. Allow to dry completely.

3. Pipe the ears using light green icing and No. 1.5 tip. Pipe the screws using gray icing and No. 1.5 tip.

4. Pipe 2 crossed lines as a bandage in the upper left side of the head using flesh icing and No. 5 tip. Pipe wavy lines on the hair using black icing and No. 1.5 tip.

5. Using a paintbrush, apply pink petal dust to the cheeks. Dip a toothpick in white edible airbrush color and paint a small dot on each cheek.

6. Draw eyebrows, a smile, and dots on the bandage using a fine black edible marker.

7. Dilute silver luster dust in a few drops of edible alcohol. Use the paintbrush to apply paint to the screws. Allow to dry. If necessary, add a second layer.

Jack-o-Lantern

The Jack-o-Lantern is one of the best-known Halloween symbols and it can be carved into many different facial expressions—usually scary. But who says Jack can't be friendly? You can adapt the design to any pumpkin cookie cutter. You can also vary the background color by using yellow instead of black to simulate internal light. *MS*

SUPPLIES

- Pumpkin cookie cutter
- Spatula
- Brown edible marker
- 3 piping bags and couplers
- Piping tips (Nos. 1.5, 3, 14)
- Round No. 4 or No. 5 paintbrush
- Pink petal dust
- Toothpick
- White edible airbrush color
- Royal icing:
  Black (honey consistency)
  Orange (honey consistency)
  Lime green (buttercream consistency)

1. Choose a basic cookie recipe on page 7, and make a batch of cookies using a pumpkin cutter. Allow the cookies to cool completely before decorating.
2. Use a spatula to spread a thin layer of black icing on the cookie. Allow to dry completely.
3. Trace the eyes and smile using a brown edible marker and the provided template (see pages 134–139).
4. Outline the eyes and smile using black icing and No. 1.5 tip.
5. Outline the pumpkin using orange icing and No. 1.5 tip. Allow to dry completely.
6. Flood the pumpkin using orange icing and No. 3 tip.
7. Pipe short lines on the top and bottom of the pumpkin as divisions.
8. Pipe the stem using lime green icing and No. 14 tip. Change the tip to No. 1.5 and pipe green spirals under the stem (see picture).
9. Use a paintbrush to apply pink petal dust to the cheeks. Dip a toothpick in white edible airbrush color and paint a small dot on each cheek.

TIPS & TRICKS

As an alternative to using the template, you could create royal icing transfers for the face features (see page 16).

Pumpkin

I make pumpkin cookies every year for Thanksgiving and Halloween parties. You can add some pumpkin spice to your cookie dough for extra seasonal flavor. *NK*

SUPPLIES

- Pumpkin cutter
- 5 piping bags
- Royal icing (regular consistency):
    Orange
    Ivory
    Brown
    Leaf green
    Dark green

1. Choose a basic cookie recipe on page 7, and make a batch of cookies using a pumpkin cutter. Allow the cookies to cool completely before decorating. Prepare the piping bags by cutting a 1–2-mm hole for piping and a 3-mm hole for flooding.

2. Outline and flood the right and left parts of the pumpkin using orange icing. While the icing is wet, pipe different sized dots on the bottom of the pumpkin using ivory icing. Allow to dry completely.

3. Flood the middle of the cookie with orange icing and add dots on the bottom of the pumpkin.

4. Pipe the pumpkin stem using ivory icing and outline it with brown icing.

5. Use leaf green and dark green icing to pipe leaves and a stem across the top of the pumpkin. Allow to dry completely.

Bat

These Halloween cookies are super simple to make, so they are perfect if you're new to cookie decorating—you don't need many supplies either. *NK*

SUPPLIES

- Bat cookie cutter
- 3 piping bags
- Royal icing (regular consistency):
  Black
  White
  Green

1. Choose a basic cookie recipe on page 7, and make a batch of cookies using a bat cutter. Allow the cookies to cool completely before decorating. Prepare the piping bags by cutting a 1–2-mm hole for piping and a 3-mm hole for flooding.

2. Outline and flood the bat using black icing. While the icing is wet, pipe white and green icing dots for the eyes.

3. Using black icing, outline the wings and the body of the bat. Pipe the mouth, ears, and a bow with black icing. Allow to dry completely.

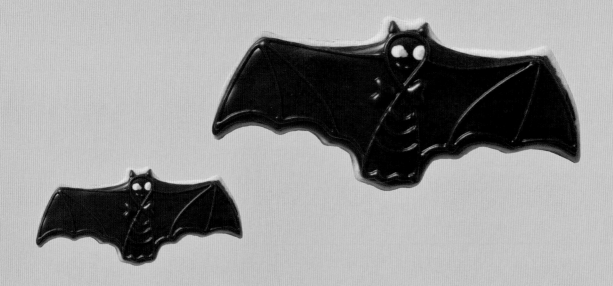

Cat

Black cats are a classic Halloween symbol, but they don't need to be scary—you can make a cute version like this one. *NK*

SUPPLIES

- Fancy plaque cutter
- 3 piping bags
- Metal skewer or toothpick
- Paintbrush
- Gold food coloring
- Royal icing (regular consistency):

    Light pink

    Black

    White

1. Choose a basic cookie recipe on page 7, and make a batch of cookies using a fancy plaque cutter. Allow the cookies to cool completely before decorating. Prepare the piping bags by cutting a 1–2-mm hole for piping and a 3-mm hole for flooding.

2. Outline and flood the cookie with light pink icing. Allow to dry completely.

3. Use black icing to pipe the cat onto the cookie. While the icing is wet, pipe white dots on the face. Use a metal skewer or toothpick to drag through the dots to make eyes. Pipe a white dot for the mouth.

4. Pipe the cat's hat and tail using black icing and allow to dry completely.

5. Outline the body and paws with black icing. Pipe the ears using black icing.

6. Use a paintbrush and gold food coloring to draw a line and dots on the hat.

7. Create a border around the cookie by piping black dots. Allow to dry completely.

Dreidel

To make this cookie, I use a nail polish cookie cutter and a sharp knife to add the extra angle to the base. *NK*

SUPPLIES

- Nail polish cookie cutter
- Knife
- 3 piping bags
- Airbrush
- Sky blue edible airbrush color
- Royal icing (regular consistency):
  - Blue
  - Yellow
  - Black

1. Choose a basic cookie recipe on page 7, and make a batch of cookies using a nail polish cutter. Before baking, use a knife to cut each cookie into a point at the base, to resemble the dreidel shape. Allow the cookies to cool completely before decorating. Prepare the piping bags by cutting a 1–2-mm hole for piping and a 3-mm hole for flooding.

2. Outline and flood the cookie using blue icing. Allow to dry completely.

3. Using an airbrush and sky blue edible airbrush color, make shadows on the 2 imaginary rectangles and the right side of the handle.

4. Outline the cookie and all parts of the dreidel with blue icing.

5. Pipe the letters with yellow icing.

6. Outline the edges of the whole cookie with black icing. Allow to dry completely.

Menorah

These Hanukkah cookies will shine brightly on any table. *NK*

1. Choose a basic cookie recipe on page 7, and make a batch of cookies using a menorah cutter. Allow the cookies to cool completely before decorating. Prepare the piping bags by cutting a 1–2-mm hole for piping and a 3-mm hole for flooding.

2. Outline and flood the base of the menorah with yellow icing. Use yellow icing to pipe the curved lines for candle holders, crossing the base of the lamp.

3. Pipe blue dots on top of each line. Using white icing, pipe white dots on the blue dots. Use a metal skewer or toothpick to drag through the white dots to make little lights.

4. Use yellow icing to outline the base, and pipe the Star of David in the middle of the menorah. Pipe 3 strokes on the bottom of the lamp base. Allow to dry completely.

SUPPLIES

- Menorah cookie cutter
- 3 piping bags
- Metal skewer or toothpick
- Royal icing (regular consistency):
  - Yellow
  - Blue
  - White

Snowflake

Red and white is a beautiful and traditional color combination for Christmas, and these snowflakes are the perfect way to celebrate. *NK*

SUPPLIES

- Snowflake cookie cutter
- 2 piping bags
- White sugar pearls
- Royal icing (regular consistency):
  Red
  White

1

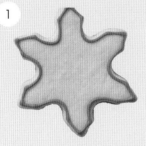

Choose a basic cookie recipe on page 7, and make a batch of cookies using a snowflake cutter. Allow the cookies to cool completely before decorating. Prepare the piping bags by cutting a 1–2-mm hole for piping and a 3-mm hole for flooding. Outline the cookie with red icing.

2

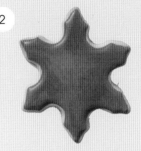

Flood the cookie with red icing. Allow to dry completely.

3

Pipe the snowflake decorations with white icing (see picture).

4

Using white icing, glue a sugar pearl in the center of the snowflake. Allow to dry completely. You can reverse the color scheme for half the batch of cookies to make a more decorative display.

5

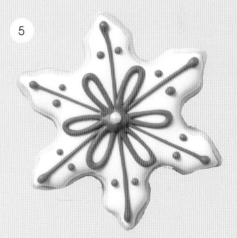

Snowman

This is another fairly easy design to master. The only tricky part is creating the wavy lines on the scarf, but with a bit of practice this will become second nature. *NK*

SUPPLIES

- Snowman cookie cutter
- 5 piping bags
- Fine black edible marker
- Metal skewer
- Royal icing (regular consistency):
  White
  Black
  Orange
  Light blue
  Royal blue

1

Choose a basic cookie recipe on page 7, and make a batch of cookies using a snowman cutter. Allow the cookies to cool completely before decorating. Prepare the piping bags by cutting a 1–2-mm hole for piping and a 3-mm hole for flooding. Outline and flood the snowman with white icing. Allow to dry.

2

Pipe the arms with white icing. Using black icing, pipe the top part of the hat and the eyes. Allow to dry.

3

Pipe the bottom of the hat. Pipe the nose using orange icing. Use a black edible marker to draw a mouth. Pipe the scarf with light blue icing and pipe lines using royal blue and white icing. Use a metal skewer to create a marble effect.

4

Using white icing, outline the bottom of the snowman with swirls on the left and right sides. Allow to dry completely.

Christmas Tree

The Christmas tree is one of the most popular symbols associated with this festive season.
Make it a happy one! MS

SUPPLIES

- Christmas tree with star cookie cutter
- 3 piping bags and couplers
- Piping tips (Nos. 1.5, 2, 3)
- Accent tweezers
- Black edible pearls
- Round No. 4 or No. 5 paintbrush
- Pink petal dust
- Toothpick
- White edible airbrush color
- Fine black edible marker
- Gold dragees
- Royal icing:

Yellow (meringue consistency)

Lime green (honey consistency)

Brown (meringue consistency)

TIPS & TRICKS

Practice on paper before you pipe the swirls on the tree. To learn how to pipe swirls, see the techniques section (page 17).

1. Choose a basic cookie recipe on page 7, and make a batch of cookies using a Christmas tree with star cutter. Allow the cookies to cool completely before decorating.

2. Outline and flood the star using yellow icing and No. 2 tip. Allow to dry for about 30 minutes.

3. Outline and flood the tree using lime green icing and No. 3 tip. While the icing is wet, use accent tweezers to add 2 black edible pearls for eyes. Allow to dry completely.

4. Outline and flood the tree trunk using brown icing and No. 2 tip. Allow to dry.

5. Use a paintbrush to apply pink petal dust to the cheeks. Dip a toothpick in white edible airbrush color and paint a small dot on each cheek. Draw eyebrows and a smile using a fine black edible marker.

6. Pipe a dot in the middle of the star using yellow icing and No. 1.5 tip. While the icing is wet, use the tweezers to add a gold dragee. Use the same icing and tip to pipe swirls on the star.

7. Pipe swirls and dots on the tree using lime green icing and No. 1.5 tip (see picture). Pipe a wavy line on the tree trunk using brown icing and no. 1.5 tip. Allow to dry completely.

Gingerbread House

Gingerbread houses are my favorite Christmas decoration. I use pastel colors, but you can be more traditional if you like. Imagine how the Christmas tree will look decorated with lots of little gingerbread houses. *MS*

SUPPLIES

- Gingerbread house cookie cutter
- 7 piping bags and couplers
- Piping tips (Nos. 1.5, 2, 3, 14)
- Multicolored nonpareils
- White edible glitter
- Yellow edible marker
- Mini heart-shaped cookie cutter
- Accent tweezers
- Colored pearls
- Royal icing:

Light brown (honey consistency)

White (buttercream consistency)

Pink (meringue consistency)

Violet (meringue consistency)

Green (meringue consistency)

Orange (meringue consistency)

White (meringue consistency)

1

Choose a basic cookie recipe on page 7, and make a batch of cookies using a gingerbread house cutter. Allow the cookies to cool completely before decorating. Outline and flood the house using light brown icing and No. 3 tip. Allow to dry completely.

2

Pipe the snow on the roof and chimney using white icing (buttercream consistency) and No. 14 tip. While the icing is wet, add multicolored nonpareils and white edible glitter. Use a yellow edible marker to trace the door. Use a mini heart-shaped cookie cutter to mark the window. Outline and flood the heart using pink icing and No. 2 tip.

3

Outline and flood the door using violet icing and No. 2 tip. While the icing is wet, use accent tweezers to add a pearl on the right side of the door. Allow to dry.

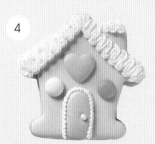

4

Change to No. 2 tip and use white icing (buttercream consistency) to pipe a wavy line around the door. Pipe a small circle just above the left side of the door using green icing and No. 2 tip. Pipe a second small circle at the right side of the door using orange icing and No. 2 tip.

5

Using white icing (meringue consistency) and No. 1.5 tip, pipe outlines on the heart and circles to create the window, lollipops, and sticks. Pipe green dots for a wreath on the door. While the icing is wet, add colored nonpareils to decorate. Pipe the snow on the bottom of the house using white icing (buttercream consistency) and No. 14 tip. Allow to dry completely.

Gingerbread Man

Decorated gingerbread men cookies are perfect to give as a gift for the holidays. Most people use a gingerbread recipe for these cookies. However, I prefer to use my basic cookie recipe with added flavors such as lemon, coconut, orange, rum, or almond. Here, I use several royal icing techniques for decorating these cookies, such as flooding, wet-on-dry, and wet-on-wet (see pages 17). *NK*

SUPPLIES

- Gingerbread man cookie cutter
- 4 piping bags
- Airbrush
- Brown edible airbrush color
- Royal icing (regular consistency):
  - Brown
  - Red
  - White
  - Blue

1. Choose a basic cookie recipe on page 7, and make a batch of cookies using a gingerbread man cutter. Allow the cookies to cool completely before decorating. Prepare the piping bags by cutting a 1–2-mm hole for piping and a 3-mm hole for flooding.

2. Outline and flood the cookie with brown icing. Allow to dry completely.

3. Use an airbrush and brown edible airbrush color to make a shadow on the cookie.

4. Pipe bows using red icing. While the icing is wet, pipe small white dots on the bows.

5. Pipe the eyes and mouth using white icing, and pipe red dots at each end of the mouth. Pipe decorative white lines around the arms and legs (see picture). Pipe 2 blue icing dots for buttons. Allow to dry completely.

Stamped Reindeer

I use the traditional holiday colors for these cookies, but you can choose whichever colors you like—the main theme is still very festive! *NK*

SUPPLIES

- Circle cookie cutter
- 3 piping bags
- Small sponge
- Deer stamp
- Black gel food color
- Red gel food color
- Green gel food color
- Gold gel food color
- Royal icing (regular consistency):
  White
  Green
  Red

1

Choose a basic cookie recipe on page 7, and make a batch of cookies using a circle cutter. Allow the cookies to cool completely before decorating. Prepare the piping bags by cutting a 1–2-mm hole for piping and a 3-mm hole for flooding. Outline and flood the cookie with white icing. Allow to dry completely.

2

Using a sponge, put black gel food color on a deer stamp. Press the stamp firmly down on the cookie to ensure the outline is even and intact.

3

Using red, green, and gold gel food colors, color the deer's body, horns, hooves, scarf, and star.

4

Make a border by piping green and red dots around the cookie. Allow to dry completely.

Elf

This fun and festive elf in a striped hat will make a colorful addition to the Christmas table. *NK*

SUPPLIES

- Ice cream cookie cutter
- 6 piping bags
- Metal skewer or toothpick
- Paintbrush
- Flamingo blossom dust
- Royal icing (regular consistency):
  - Red
  - Fuchsia
  - Tan
  - Black
  - White
  - Brown

TIPS & TRICKS

Allow the red stripes on the hat to dry completely before piping the fuchsia stripes to avoid blending the colors.

1 Choose a basic cookie recipe on page 7, and make a batch of cookies using an ice cream cutter. Allow the cookies to cool completely before decorating. Prepare the piping bags by cutting a 1–2-mm hole for piping and a 3-mm hole for flooding. Outline the hat and stripes using red icing. Flood the stripes with red icing.

2 Flood the empty sections with fuchsia icing.

3 Outline and flood the face using tan icing. While the icing is wet, pipe 2 big black dots, then 2 white dots and 2 more black dots for eyes. Use black icing and a metal skewer or toothpick to create a mouth.

4 Flood the fur on the hat using white icing. Pipe a tassel using white icing. Pipe the nose using tan icing. Using a paintbrush and flamingo blossom dust, draw cheeks on the face.

5 Pipe the hair and brows using brown icing. Outline the hat with white and red icing. Allow to dry completely.

Reindeer

This sparkly reindeer looks very festive and can be used as a table decoration or to decorate your tree. *MS*

SUPPLIES

- Reindeer cookie cutter
- Yellow edible marker
- 5 piping bags and couplers
- Piping tips (Nos. 1.5, 2, 3)
- White sanding sugar
- Round No. 4 or No. 5 paintbrush
- Pink petal dust
- Toothpick
- White edible airbrush color
- Fine black edible marker
- Royal icing:
  Ivory (honey consistency)
  Brown (meringue consistency)
  Pink (meringue consistency)
  White (meringue consistency)
  Red (meringue consistency)

1. Choose a basic cookie recipe on page 7, and make a batch of cookies using a reindeer cutter. Allow the cookies to cool completely before decorating.

2. Trace the reindeer onto the cookie using a yellow edible marker.

3. Outline and flood the head using ivory icing and No. 3 tip. Allow to dry for about 30 minutes.

4. Outline and flood the reindeer horns using brown icing and No. 2 tip. Outline and fill the ears using ivory icing and No. 2 tip. While the icing is wet, pipe the inner ears, using pink icing and No. 1.5 tip. Allow to dry.

5. Outline and flood one part of the scarf using white icing and No. 3 tip. While the icing is wet, pour white sanding sugar over the scarf and allow to dry for about 30 minutes. Follow the same procedure for the second part.

6. Pipe an oval shape for the nose using red icing and No. 2 tip. Pipe snow onto the horns using white icing and No. 1.5 tip.

7. Using a paintbrush, apply pink petal dust to the cheeks. Dip a toothpick in white edible airbrush color and paint a small dot on each cheek. Draw eyebrows and eyes using a fine black edible marker. Allow to dry completely.

Santa

There are a lot of beautiful designs for Santa cookies, so I've tried to make something a little different. I hope you agree that it's an easy cookie to make and looks cute. *NK*

SUPPLIES

- Santa face cookie cutter
- 5 piping bags
- Piping tip (No. 16)
- Paintbrush
- Flamingo blossom dust
- Royal icing:

  Red (regular consistency)

  White (regular consistency)

  White (thick consistency)

  Tan (regular consistency)

  Black (regular consistency)

1

Choose a basic cookie recipe on page 7, and make a batch of cookies using a Santa face cutter. Allow the cookies to cool completely before decorating. Prepare the piping bags that don't require tips by cutting a 1–2-mm hole for piping and a 3-mm hole for flooding (cut a smaller hole for the beard). Outline the hat with red icing and the beard with white icing (regular consistency).

2

Flood the hat using red icing and pipe the face using tan icing. Allow to dry. Pipe black dots for eyes.

3

Flood the beard using white icing (regular consistency).

4

Using white icing (thick consistency) and No. 16 tip, pipe the fur on the hat. Pipe the snowflakes, mustache, and brows with white icing. To pipe the curls on the beard, use white icing (thick consistency) and a piping bag with the smallest hole you can make. Using a paintbrush and flamingo blossom dust, draw the cheeks on Santa's face. Using tan icing, pipe a big dot for the nose. Allow to dry completely.

Santa Hat

In just a few easy steps you can make this eye-catching Santa hat. *MS*

SUPPLIES

- Santa's hat cookie cutter
- 2 piping bags and couplers
- Piping tip (no. 3)
- Airbrush
- Holiday red edible airbrush color
- Brown edible airbrush color
- White nonpareils
- Accent tweezers
- Berry and holly leaf sprinkles
- Royal icing (honey consistency):
  - Tulip red
  - White

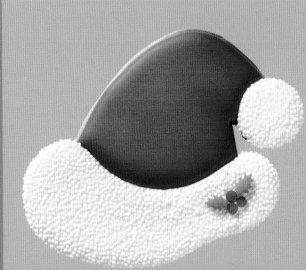

1. Choose a basic cookie recipe on page 7, and make a batch of cookies using a Santa's hat cutter. Allow the cookies to cool completely before decorating.

2. Outline and flood the hat using tulip red icing and No. 3 tip. Allow to dry completely.

3. Using an airbrush and a mix of holiday red and brown edible airbrush colors, airbrush the edges of the hat. Allow to dry completely.

4. Outline and flood the tassel using white icing and No. 3 tip. While the icing is wet, quickly pour white nonpareils on the tassel. Allow to dry completely.

5. Outline and flood the fur edges using white icing and No. 3 tip. While the icing is wet, quickly pour white nonpareils on the fur edges. Allow to dry completely.

6. Pipe a dot of white icing on the right side of the hat and use tweezers to glue berry and holly leaf sprinkles on the fur.

TIPS & TRICKS

If you don't have an airbrush, use a paintbrush and brown petal dust to apply the shade. Or, simply outline the hat using the same red royal icing and No. 1.5 tip.

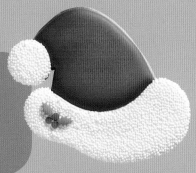

SPECIAL OCCASIONS

Bunch of Balloons

These fun, colorful cookies are perfect for parties—you could even let the kids decorate them as part of the activities. To make these, I use the wet-on-wet, and wet-on-dry techniques (see page 17). *NK*

SUPPLIES

- Scalloped oval cookie cutter
- 9 piping bags
- Royal icing (regular consistency):
  - White
  - Black
  - Green
  - Red
  - Yellow
  - Sky blue
  - Royal blue
  - Pink
  - Fuchsia

1

Choose a basic cookie recipe on page 7, and make a batch of cookies using a scalloped oval cutter. Allow the cookies to cool completely before decorating. Prepare the piping bags by cutting a 1–2-mm hole for piping and a 3-mm hole for flooding. Outline and flood the cookie with white icing.

2

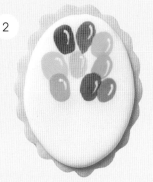

While the icing is wet, pipe the balloons onto the cookie using all the different icing colors. Immediately pipe the highlights with white icing.

3

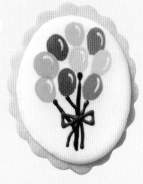

Pipe the balloon strings and a bow with black icing.

4

Pipe a border around the edge of the cookie with white icing. Allow to dry completely.

Fireworks

These versatile cookies are great for any party or celebration. The marbled effect makes them look especially realistic. *NK*

SUPPLIES

- Circle cookie cutter
- 6 piping bags
- Metal skewer or toothpick
- Edible disco dust
- Royal icing (regular consistency):

  Violet

  White

  Red

  Yellow

  Pink

  Black

1

Choose a basic cookie recipe on page 7, and make a batch of cookies using a circle cutter. Allow the cookies to cool completely before decorating. Prepare the piping bags by cutting a 1–2-mm hole for piping and a 3-mm hole for flooding. Outline and flood the outer part of the circle with violet icing.

2

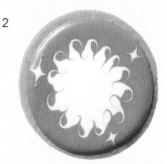

While the icing is wet, fill the middle with white icing. Drag a metal skewer or toothpick through the violet and white icing to create a marbled effect. Pipe 3 white dots around the cookie and drag the skewer through the dots to make stars. Allow to dry completely.

3

Pipe the firework traces in curved lines, using red, yellow, and pink icing. Pipe little dots around the cookie with yellow, and pink icing. While the icing is wet, sprinkle edible disco dust over the cookie. Allow to dry.

4

Pipe the border with black icing by making little dots around the cookie. Allow to dry completely.

Graduation Cap

This cookie is a popular favor at graduation parties. I use blue icing to decorate it but you can choose the color that best matches your celebration. *MS*

Bon Voyage

I often use the same cookie cutter for different designs. A cake cutter works perfectly for these bon voyage cookies. *NK*

SUPPLIES

- Graduation cap cookie cutter
- Yellow edible marker
- 3 piping bags and couplers
  - Piping tips (Nos. 1.5, 2)
  - Scribe tool or toothpick
  - Royal icing:

Light and medium royal blue (honey consistency)

Egg yellow (buttercream consistency)

1. Choose a basic cookie recipe on page 7, and make a batch of cookies using a graduation cap cutter. Allow the cookies to cool completely before decorating.
2. Using a yellow edible marker, divide the diamond shape of the cap.
3. Outline the cap in medium royal blue icing and No. 2 tip. Allow to dry.
4. Flood the diamond shape in medium royal blue icing and No. 2 tip. Immediately pipe a line at the bottom of the diamond with the lighter shade of royal blue icing using No. 2 tip. If needed, you can shake the cookie carefully to help the colors blend.
5. Change to No. 1.5 tip and flood the bottom of the cap with medium royal blue icing. Allow to dry.
6. Pipe a dot in the center of the diamond with medium royal blue icing and No. 1.5 tip. Allow to dry.
7. Using egg yellow icing and No. 2 tip, pipe a zigzag line to look like rope. Finish the line just before the lower knot zone.
8. Pipe a big dot in egg yellow icing and let it crust before piping a half circle just below it.
9. At the end of the tassel, pipe lines, using egg yellow icing and No. 1.5 tip. Pipe more lines between the first ones to add volume.

SUPPLIES

- Cake cookie cutter
  - 4 piping bags
    - Airbrush
  - Brown edible airbrush color
  - Paintbrush
- Silver food color
- Red edible marker
- Royal icing (regular consistency):

Brown

Violet

Black

White

1. Choose a basic cookie recipe on page 7, and make a batch of cookies using a cake cookie cutter. Allow to cool completely before decorating. Prepare the piping bags by cutting a 1–2-mm hole for piping and a 3-mm hole for flooding.
2. Outline and flood the bottom suitcase with brown icing.
3. Outline and flood the middle case with violet icing.
4. Outline and flood the top case with black icing. Allow to dry completely.
5. Using an airbrush and brown edible airbrush color, spray the edges of the bottom case.
6. Pipe the black lines, handle, and corners of the top case, using black icing. Pipe the brown handle, lines, and corners on the bottom case using brown icing. Pipe the tag with white icing. Pipe the lines on the middle case with violet icing, then add straps and a handle using brown icing. Pipe the clips and locks on all the cases with violet icing. Allow to dry completely.
7. Using a paintbrush and silver food color, paint all the clips and locks to make them look like metal. Use a red edible marker to write the name on the tag. Pipe black dots on the straps with black icing. Allow to dry completely.

Party Popper

Party poppers let everyone know you're having a great time, and this cookie will add the same element of celebration to any occasion. *MS*

SUPPLIES

- 2¾-in (7-cm) fluted edge square cookie cutter
- Smaller square cookie cutter
- Yellow edible marker
- 5 piping bags and couplers
- Piping tips (Nos. 1.5, 2, 3)
- Accent tweezers
- Star sprinkles
- Scribe tool or toothpick
- Royal icing:
  White (honey consistency)
  Orange (meringue consistency)
  Yellow (meringue consistency)
  Pink (meringue consistency)
  Green (meringue consistency)

1. Choose a basic cookie recipe on page 7, and make a batch of cookies using a fluted edge square cutter. Allow the cookies to cool completely before decorating.

2. Using a smaller square cookie cutter and a yellow edible marker, trace a square onto the cookie as a guide to fill the background.

3. Using white icing and No. 3 tip, outline and flood the inner square. Allow to dry completely.

4. Trace the party popper using the yellow edible marker and the provided template (see pages 134–139).

5. Outline and fill the party popper using orange icing and No. 2 tip. While the icing is wet, pipe slanted lines across the horn using yellow icing and No. 1.5 tip. Allow to dry.

6. Use tweezers and dots of white icing to glue star sprinkles to the cookie.

7. Using different icing colors and No. 1.5 tip, pipe swirls and dots as decorations above the party popper (see picture).

8. Pipe dots around the fluted edge of the cookie to create a border using different icing colors and No. 1.5 tip.

Occasion Cake

This cake was inspired by simply colored fondant cakes. I use some of my favorite colors here, but you can choose your own favorites or pick colors to match the celebration. *MS*

SUPPLIES

- Cake cookie cutter
- Pink royal icing flower transfers
- Yellow edible marker
- 5 piping bags and couplers
- Piping tips (Nos. 1.5, 2, 3, 46)
- Scribe tool or toothpick
- Accent tweezers
- Royal icing:

Pink (honey consistency)

White (honey consistency)

Blue (honey consistency)

Green (honey consistency)

Burgundy (buttercream consistency)

1. Choose a basic cookie recipe on page 7, and make a batch of cookies using a cake cutter. Allow the cookies to cool completely before decorating.

2. Make the icing flower transfers in advance (see page 17).

3. Use a yellow edible marker to trace each cake tier. Outline and flood the base of the cake using pink icing and No. 3 tip. While the icing is wet, pipe dots evenly across the base using white icing and No. 1.5 tip. If necessary, use a scribe tool or toothpick to merge the colors. It is not necessary to let it dry completely.

4. Outline and flood the middle tier of the cake using blue icing and No. 3 tip. While the icing is wet, pipe dots using pink icing and No. 1.5 tip. If necessary, use a scribe tool or toothpick to merge the colors.

5. Outline and flood the top tier using green icing and No. 2 tip. While the icing is wet, pipe dots using pink icing and No. 1.5 tip. If necessary, use the scribe tool or toothpick to merge the colors. Allow to dry completely.

6. Pipe horizontal lines as ribbons (one at a time) onto each tier division using burgundy icing and No. 46 tip. While the icing is wet, use accent tweezers to add an icing flower on each line (see picture). Pipe drops and dots as details in every tier corner using the same icing base color and No. 1.5 tip. Pipe pink dots along the base of the cake using the same icing color and tip.

Ring

Diamond ring cookies are the perfect favor at engagement parties, and the diamond is the most visible detail on this cookie. An alternative is to make the diamond in one piece and when it is completely dry, pipe thin lines onto the diamond to define the facets. *MS*

SUPPLIES

- Ring cookie cutter
- Yellow edible marker
- 4 piping bags and couplers
- Piping tips (Nos. 1.5, 2)
- Accent tweezers
- Mini silver dragees
- Round No. 4 or No. 5 paintbrush
- White luster dust
- Royal icing:

White (meringue consistency)

Light and medium pastel pink or blue (meringue consistency)

White (honey consistency)

1. Choose a basic cookie recipe on page 7, and make a batch of cookies using a ring cutter. Allow the cookies to cool completely before decorating.

2. Trace the diamond and ring onto the cookie using a yellow edible marker.

3. Pipe the diamond outlines using white icing (meringue consistency) and No. 1.5 tip. Allow to dry for about 30 minutes.

4. Carefully fill some of the diamond sections using light pastel pink or blue icing and No. 1.5 tip. Allow to dry for 30 minutes. Fill the adjacent sections with medium pink or blue icing, and continue until the diamond is complete.

5. Outline the ring using white icing (honey consistency) and No. 1.5 tip. Immediately fill the ring using the same royal icing and No. 2 tip. Allow to dry.

6. Pipe a dot onto each diamond intersection and use accent tweezers to apply mini silver dragees.

7. Pipe the ring swirls and dots using white icing (meringue consistency) and No. 1.5 tip (see picture). Allow to dry completely.

8. When the diamond is completely dry, use a paintbrush to apply white luster dust to make it shine.

TIPS & TRICKS
You can use circle cookie cutters to trace the ring perfectly round.

Champagne Glass

Champagne glass cookies are often made for engagement parties, but they also make a lovely New Year dinner table centerpiece. *NK*

SUPPLIES

- Champagne glass cookie cutter
- 2 piping bags
- Airbrush
- Orange edible airbrush color
- Pearl edible airbrush color
- Yellow sanding sugar
- Satin bows
- Royal icing (regular consistency):
  Gold
  White

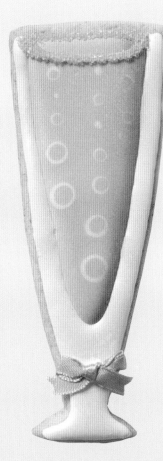

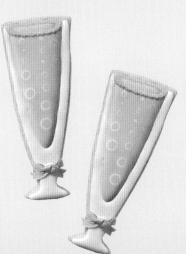

1. Choose a basic cookie recipe on page 7, and make a batch of cookies using a Champagne glass cutter. Allow the cookies to cool completely before decorating. Prepare the piping bags by cutting a 1–2-mm hole for piping and a 3-mm hole for flooding.

2. Outline and flood the Champagne section with gold icing. While the icing is wet, pipe white dots, then pipe gold dots on top to resemble bubbles. Allow to dry completely.

3. Using an airbrush and orange edible airbrush color, make shadows on the right side of the cookie.

4. Outline and flood the glass with white icing. Allow to dry completely.

5. Using the airbrush and pearl edible airbrush color, spray the whole cookie. Outline the top part of the glass with gold icing. While the icing is wet, sprinkle with yellow sanding sugar.

6. Add a satin bow on the bottom of the cookie using white icing to glue into place. Allow to dry completely.

Heart

The special person in your life will love these elegant white-on-white icing heart cookies. They would also make a lovely addition to a bridal shower or wedding reception. *NK*

Silhouette

This elegant cookie of a bride and groom silhouette will make a lovely gift for a newly engaged or married couple. *MS*

SUPPLIES

- Heart cookie cutter
- 2 piping bags
- Piping tips (Nos. 16, 352)
- Royal icing:
  White (thick consistency)
  White (regular consistency)

1. Choose a basic cookie recipe on page 7, and make a batch of cookies using a heart cutter. Allow the cookies to cool completely before decorating. Prepare the piping bags that don't require tips by cutting a 1–2-mm hole for piping and a 3-mm hole for flooding.

2. Outline and flood the heart with white icing (regular). Allow to dry completely.

3. Using No. 16 tip and white icing (thick), pipe the decorations. Begin by keeping the tip perpendicular to the cookie, hovering above it. Pipe a small spiral in the center of the heart to create a rose. Make 2 more swirl roses on the top part of the cookie (see page 17).

4. Using No. 352 tip, pipe a leaf under each rose. Pipe lace decorations around the heart—scallops, dots, and ruffles—using white icing (see picture). Allow to dry completely.

SUPPLIES

- 2¾- x 3-in (7- x 8-cm) heart cookie cutter
- 4 piping bags and couplers
- Piping tips (Nos. 1.5, 2, 3)
- Pink edible marker (or any light color)
- Royal icing:
  White (honey consistency)
  Burgundy (honey consistency)
  Pink (buttercream consistency)
  Lime green (buttercream consistency)

1. Choose a basic cookie recipe on page 7, and make a batch of cookies using a heart cutter. Allow the cookies to cool completely before decorating.

2. Outline and flood the cookie using white icing and No. 3 tip. Allow to dry completely.

3. Trace the silhouette couple with a pink edible marker, using the provided template (see pages 134–139).

4. Outline and fill the silhouette couple using burgundy icing and No. 1.5 tip. Allow to dry.

5. Pipe a white garland with white icing and No. 1.5 tip. Pipe a few white dots around the border. Allow to dry.

6. Pipe 4 small swirl roses (see page 17) using pink icing and No. 1.5 tip. Pipe 2 leaves around each rose, using lime green icing and No. 1.5 tip.

Wedding Dress

This is one of my favorite cookie cutters, as I love making cookie dresses. Bake a batch of dress cookies using your favorite recipe and you can decorate them for different occasions. *NK*

SUPPLIES
- Dress cookie cutter
- 2 piping bags
- Pink and white edible pearls
- Royal icing:
  White (regular consistency)
  White (thick consistency)

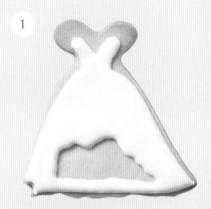

1. Choose a basic cookie recipe on page 7, and make a batch of cookies using a dress cutter. Allow the cookies to cool completely before decorating. Prepare the piping bags by cutting a 1–2-mm hole for piping and a 3-mm hole for flooding. Outline and flood the dress using white icing (regular consistency).

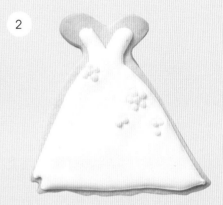

2. While the icing is wet, add edible pearls to decorate the dress (see picture). Allow to dry completely.

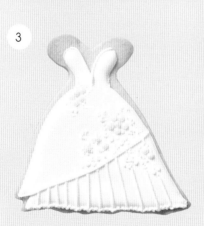

3. Pipe the details, lines, and dots on the bottom of the dress using white icing (thick consistency).

4. Pipe the lace on the top of the dress with white icing (thick consistency) and allow to dry completely.

Tux Jacket

These cookies will be great little favors for wedding guests, especially when paired with the Wedding Dress cookie. You can add extra decorations if you like. *NK*

SUPPLIES

- Sweater cookie cutter
- 4 piping bags
- Piping tip (No. 65s)
- Pearl food color spray
- Royal icing (regular consistency):
  - White
  - Black
  - Green
  - Pink

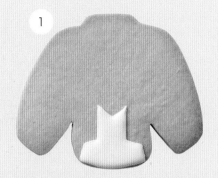

1

Choose a basic cookie recipe on page 7, and make a batch of cookies using a sweater cutter. Allow the cookies to cool completely before decorating. Prepare the piping bags that don't require tips by cutting a 1–2-mm hole for piping and a 3-mm hole for flooding. Outline and flood the bottom of the jacket with white icing.

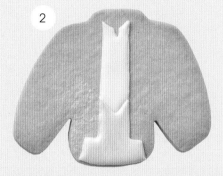

2

Spray pearl food color spray over the jacket. Pipe the visible part of the shirt with white icing.

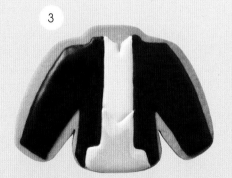

3

Outline and flood the jacket with black icing. Allow to dry completely.

4

Outline the collar and the front part of the jacket with black icing. Pipe the bow tie, buttons on the shirt, and jacket with black icing. Using white icing, pipe the buttons on the lower part of the jacket and a rose on the collar. Using green icing and No. 65s tip, pipe tiny leaves around the rose. Add tiny pink dots around the rose. Allow to dry completely.

Bride & Groom

This cookie would also make a cute cake topper for a wedding reception. 𝓝𝓚

SUPPLIES

- Bride and groom cookie cutter
- 7 piping bags
- Royal icing face transfers (see page 17)
- Royal icing (regular consistency):
  - White
  - Tan
  - Black
  - Dark green
  - Light yellow
  - Pink
  - Fuchsia

1

Choose a basic cookie recipe on page 7, and make a batch of cookies using a bride and groom cutter. Allow the cookies to cool completely before decorating. Prepare the piping bags by cutting a 1–2-mm hole for piping and a 3-mm hole for flooding. Outline and flood the veil with white icing. Pipe the faces with tan icing. While the icing is wet, use white icing to apply face transfers onto the bride and groom.

2

Outline and flood the dress with white icing, the jacket and hat with black icing, and the pants with dark green icing.

3

Pipe the hair with light yellow icing and the arms using tan icing. Outline the groom's outfit with black and dark green icing.

4

Pipe the details onto the dress using white icing (see picture). Add the bouquet and the flowers to the hat using dark green, pink, fuchsia, and light yellow icing. Allow to dry completely.

Wedding Cake

Wedding cake cookies are usually made to look like a real wedding cake with similar designs and colors. While the tiers and shape of this cookie look like a traditional wedding cake, the bright pink color gives it a fun, modern look. *NK*

SUPPLIES

- Cake cutter
- 5 piping bags
- Royal icing:

Fuchsia (regular consistency)

Light pink (regular consistency)

Dark pink (regular consistency)

White (regular consistency)

White (thick consistency)

1. Choose a basic cookie recipe on page 7, and make a batch of cookies using a cake cutter. Allow the cookies to cool completely before decorating. Prepare the piping bags by cutting a 1–2-mm hole for piping and a 3-mm hole for flooding.

2. Outline and flood all 3 layers of the cake using fuchsia, light pink, and dark pink icing, starting at the bottom of the cake. Allow to dry completely.

3. Pipe white swirl roses (see page 17) on the cake topper. Pipe 2 swirl roses and white icing leaves on the bottom layer of the cake (see picture). Allow to dry.

4. Outline and flood the base with white icing (regular consistency). Pipe the white dots on the cake topper.

5. Pipe the garlands on the top and bottom layers of the cake, using white icing (thick consistency. Pipe the beading on the base (see picture).

6. Pipe the vertical lines on the middle layer of the cake using light pink icing. Allow to dry completely.

Confetti

For these cookies I have used a heart with wings cutter. This is a very simple but effective design that is easy to make—ideal for the novice cookie decorator. *NK*

SUPPLIES

- Heart with wings cookie cutter
- 5 piping bags
- Sprinkles
- Royal icing (regular consistency):

  White

  Green

  Red

  Yellow

  Blue

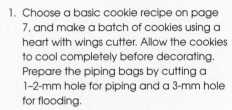

1. Choose a basic cookie recipe on page 7, and make a batch of cookies using a heart with wings cutter. Allow the cookies to cool completely before decorating. Prepare the piping bags by cutting a 1–2-mm hole for piping and a 3-mm hole for flooding.

2. Outline and flood the cookie with white icing.

3. While the icing is wet, pipe the serpentine with green icing, working across the length of the cookie.

4. While the icing is wet, put sprinkles around the serpentine. Allow to dry completely.

5. Pipe the little dots with red, yellow, green, and blue icing. Allow to dry completely.

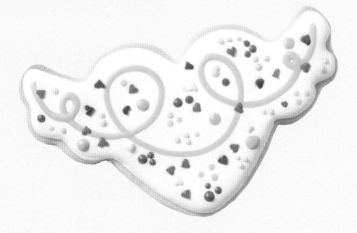

First Dance

Cookie stamping is an option if you want to decorate a simple but elegant cookie. You can use any plaque cookie cutter of your choice. *MS*

SUPPLIES

- Large scalloped oval cookie cutter (approx. 5⅛ x 3½ in/13 x 9 cm)
- Pink royal icing flower transfers
- 4 piping bags and couplers
- Piping tips (Nos. 1.5, 2, 3)
- Gold edible airbrush color
- Foam roller
- A couple stamp
- Royal icing:

White (meringue consistency)

White (10-second consistency)

White (buttercream consistency)

Pastel green (buttercream consistency)

1. Choose a basic cookie recipe on page 7, and make a batch of cookies using a large scalloped oval cutter. Allow the cookies to cool completely before decorating.

2. Make the icing flower transfers in advance (see page 17).

3. Outline the cookie using white icing (meringue consistency) and No. 2 tip. Allow to dry.

4. Flood the cookie using white icing (10-second consistency) and No. 3 tip. Allow to dry for 24 hours before stamping (to make sure the cookies have an even surface so the stamp is complete).

5. Add gold edible airbrush color to a foam roller and roll over the stamp. Stamp the icing, pressing down all over to transfer the design. Allow to dry.

6. Pipe a wavy line around the edge of the cookie using white icing (buttercream consistency) and No. 1.5 tip.

7. Glue 3 icing flower transfers under the stamped couple using white icing (meringue consistency).

8. Pipe wavy lines for leaves among the flowers using pastel green icing and No. 1.5 tip.

9. Finish the cookie by piping decorative dots (see picture). Use white icing (meringue consistency) and No. 1.5 tip.

Bride's Bouquet

For this cookie I use royal icing flower transfers made ahead of time (see page 17), and I use a No. 59 tip from Wilton. I also use small swirl roses (see page 17) to decorate the cookies. *NK*

SUPPLIES

- Mirror cookie cutter
- 5 piping bags
  - Piping tip (No. 65s)
  - Knife
- Royal icing flower transfers
  - Royal icing (regular consistency):
    White
    Leaf green
    Blue
    Dark green

1. Choose a basic cookie recipe on page 7, and make a batch of cookies using a mirror cutter. Before baking, trim the bottom off the mirror. Allow the cookies to cool completely before decorating. Prepare the piping bags that don't require tips by cutting a 1–2-mm hole for piping and a 3-mm hole for flooding.
2. Make the icing flower transfers in advance (see page 17).
3. Outline and flood the bouquet with white icing. While the icing is wet, add the icing flower transfers and pipe swirl roses (see page 17). Pipe green leaves using leaf green icing. Allow to dry completely.
4. Pipe a small leaf around each rose using a No. 65s tip and leaf green icing.
5. Pipe blue dots and pipe a border around the bouquet using dark green icing. Pipe stems on the bouquet using dark green icing.
6. Using white icing, pipe the bow on top of the stems. Allow to dry completely.

Perfect Pair

Hearts are my favorite shapes for cookies. These lovebirds will be perfect not only for weddings and anniversaries, but also for Valentine's Day. *NK*

SUPPLIES

- Heart cookie cutter
- Red edible marker
  - 3 piping bags
    - Royal icing:
    Red (regular consistency)
    White (regular consistency)
    White (thick consistency)

1. Choose a basic cookie recipe on page 7, and make a batch of cookies using a heart cutter. Allow the cookies to cool completely before decorating. Prepare the piping bags by cutting a 1–2-mm hole for piping and a 3-mm hole for flooding.
2. Draw the outlines of the birds using a red edible marker.
3. Outline and flood the heart with red icing.
4. Flood the birds with white icing (regular consistency) and allow to dry completely.
5. Outline the heart using red icing. Outline the feathers and birds with white icing.
6. Pipe red dots for eyes and add lines above the eyes with white icing (thick consistency). Allow to dry.

Teddy Bear

Teddy bears are an ideal baby shower favor. If you know the gender of the baby you can adjust the colors accordingly. *MS*

SUPPLIES

- Teddy bear cookie cutter
- Yellow edible marker
- 3 piping bags and couplers
- Piping tips (Nos. 1.5, 2, 3)
- Accent tweezers
- Black edible pearls (⅛ in/4 mm)
- Round No. 4 and No. 5 paintbrushes
- Pink petal dust
- Brown petal dust
- Toothpick
- White edible airbrush color
- Fine black edible marker
- Royal icing:
Light brown (honey consistency)
Pink (meringue consistency)
Black (meringue consistency)

1

Choose a basic cookie recipe on page 7, and make a batch of cookies using a teddy bear cutter. Allow the cookies to cool completely before decorating. Use a yellow edible marker to trace the divisions. Outline and flood the head using light brown icing and No. 2 tip. While the icing

2

Pipe the ears using light brown icing and No. 3 tip. While the icing is wet, pipe a dot inside each ear using pink icing and No. 2 tip. Allow to dry.

3

Pipe the tummy with brown icing and No. 3 tip. Outline a circle inside and fill it with pink icing using the same tip. Allow to dry.

4

Outline and flood the arms using brown icing and No. 2 tip.

5

Outline and flood the legs using the same icing and tip. Pipe the snout using pink icing and No. 2 tip.

6

Use a No. 4 paintbrush to apply pink petal dust on the cheeks. Use a No. 5 paintbrush to apply brown petal dust on the edges. Dip a toothpick in white edible airbrush color and paint dots on the cheeks. Draw eyebrows with a black edible marker. Pipe the nose using black icing and No. 1.5 tip.

Gender Reveal

A gender reveal party is a beautiful celebration where you can invite your loved ones to learn the gender of your new baby. I make this cookie in yellow, but you can choose whichever color you like. 𝓜𝓢

SUPPLIES

- Onesie cookie cutter
- Spatula
- Yellow edible marker
- 5 piping bags and couplers
- Piping tips (Nos. 1.5, 2, 3, 5)
- Accent tweezers
- Mini gold dragees
- Royal icing:
  Pink or blue (meringue consistency)
  Yellow (meringue consistency)
  Yellow (10-second consistency)
  White (10-second consistency)
  White (meringue consistency)

1

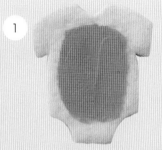

Choose a basic cookie recipe on page 7, and make a batch of cookies using a onesie cutter. Allow the cookies to cool completely before decorating. Use a spatula to spread a thick layer of pink or blue icing in the center of the cookie for the gender reveal. Allow to dry.

2

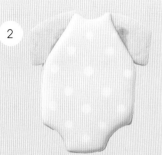

Use a yellow edible marker to divide the body and sleeves. Outline the body using yellow icing (meringue consistency) and No. 2 tip. Flood the body using yellow icing (10-second consistency) and No. 3 tip. While the icing is wet, pipe dots on the body using white icing (10-second consistency) and No. 2 tip. Allow to dry.

3

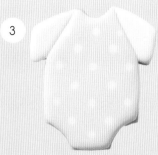

Outline and flood the sleeves using white icing (meringue consistency) and No. 2 tip. Allow to dry.

4

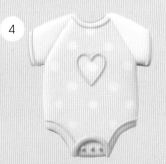

Use the marker to trace a heart on the chest. Pipe a curved line at the bottom of the onesie using yellow icing (meringue consistency) and No. 5 tip. Use No. 1.5 tip to pipe 2 lines at the neck, sleeves, and just one on the legs. Pipe 3 dots at the bottom as buttons. While the icing is wet, add mini gold dragees on each one. Pipe the heart. Let it dry.

5

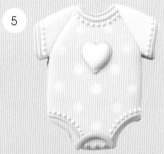

Fill the heart using white icing (meringue consistency) and No. 1.5 tip. With the same icing, pipe decorative dots around the neck, sleeves, and legs. Allow to dry completely.

Baby Bottle

Based on this set of colors, the design on the bottle is very simple. You can create a more complex bottle by including the chick. *NK*

SUPPLIES

- Baby bottle cutter
- 10 piping bags
- Royal icing (regular consistency):
  - Royal blue
  - Sky blue
  - Fuchsia
  - White
  - Light and dark pink
  - Ivory
  - Yellow
  - Black
  - Orange

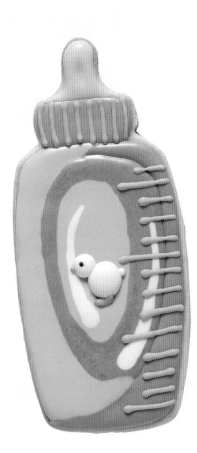

1. Choose a basic cookie recipe on page 7, and make a batch of cookies using a baby bottle cutter. Allow the cookies to cool completely before decorating. Prepare the piping bags by cutting a 1–2-mm hole for piping and a 3-mm hole for flooding.

2. Flood the base of the cookie with 3 colors (royal blue, sky blue, and fuchsia), to create a glass effect. Each color should be applied immediately after the last.

3. Use white icing to pipe 2 lines down the bottle to look like sun glare. Pipe short horizontal lines for measures using light pink icing. Allow to dry.

4. Flood the bottle cap with dark pink icing and pipe lines down the cap with light pink icing. Allow to dry.

5. Use ivory icing to pipe the nipple on the bottle and allow to dry.

6. After drying, pipe a little chick, and its feet, beak, and eyes using yellow, black, and orange icing. Allow to dry completely.

Rubber Duck

These little ducks are very popular with kids and can be made for baby showers or birthday parties. *NK*

SUPPLIES

- Rubber duck cookie cutter
- 4 piping bags
- Royal icing (regular consistency):
  Yellow
  Black
  White
  Orange

TIPS & TRICKS

If you prefer, you can use a royal icing transfer eye (see page 17). That way, each eye will be exactly the same shape and size.

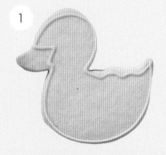

1

Choose a basic cookie recipe on page 7, and make a batch of cookies using a rubber duck cutter. Allow the cookies to cool completely before decorating. Prepare the piping bags by cutting a 1–2-mm hole for piping and a 3-mm hole for flooding. Outline the duck with yellow icing. Allow to dry.

2

Flood the duck with yellow icing, leaving the beak. Allow to dry.

3

Pipe a black dot on the head for an eye. While the icing is wet, pipe a smaller white dot on it. Flood the beak with orange icing and allow to dry completely. Outline and flood the wing with yellow icing.

4

Pipe the details on the beak and wing using white icing (see picture). Allow to dry completely.

5

Add white icing bubbles at the bottom of the duck using white icing. Allow to dry completely.

Owl

These owl cookies are made with a tulip cookie cutter, which provides the perfect outline.
This is a serious looking owl, but he's made cheerful with bright colors and fun detailing. *NK*

SUPPLIES

- Tulip cookie cutter
- 5 piping bags
- Knife
- Metal skewer or toothpick
- Royal icing (regular consistency):
  - Purple
  - Yellow
  - White
  - Fuchsia
  - Black

1

Choose a basic cookie recipe on page 7, and make a batch of cookies using a tulip cutter. Before baking, trim the stems from the tulips. Allow the cookies to cool completely before decorating. Prepare the piping bags by cutting a 1–2-mm hole for piping and a 3-mm hole for flooding. Outline the owl body using purple icing.

2

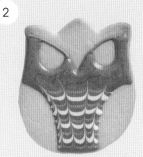

Flood the body using purple icing. Pipe horizontal lines on the body using yellow and white icing. Use a metal skewer or toothpick to drag through the lines to create a wavy effect. Allow to dry.

3

Flood the wings and head with yellow icing. Use fuchsia icing to pipe an outline of the owl's eyes.

4

Use white and black icing to pipe the rest of the eyes, and add white dots on the forehead.

5

Outline the forehead and wings with yellow icing. Pipe 2 thin vertical lines on each of the wings. Allow to dry completely.

Cow Jumped Over the Moon

This beautiful cookie will make a unique addition to a baby shower. You can adjust the colors according to your event or use pastel shades for a variation. *MS*

SUPPLIES

- 3½-in (9-cm) round cookie cutter
- Yellow edible marker
- 7 piping bags and couplers
- Piping tips (Nos. 1.5, 2, 3, 14)
- Brown edible marker
- Accent tweezers
- Black nonpareils
- Round No. 4 paintbrush
- Pink petal dust
- Fine black edible marker
- Royal icing:
  Light and medium egg yellow (honey consistency)
  Royal blue (honey consistency)
  Black (honey consistency)
  White (honey consistency)
  Flesh (meringue consistency)
  Brown (buttercream consistency)

1

Choose a basic cookie recipe on page 7, and make a batch of cookies using a round cutter. Allow the cookies to cool completely before decorating. Use a yellow edible marker to draw a curved line for the moon. Outline and flood the moon using medium egg yellow icing and No. 3 tip. Pipe dots using light egg yellow icing and No. 2 tip.

2

Flood the sky using royal blue icing and No. 3 tip. Allow to dry.

3

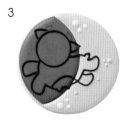

Trace the cow using a brown edible marker and the provided template (see pages 134–139). Outline the cow with black icing and No. 1.5 tip.

4

Flood the head using white icing and No. 1.5 tip. While the icing is wet, pipe spots using black icing and No. 1.5 tip. Flood 2 legs using white icing and No. 1.5 tip. While the icing is wet, pipe the hooves using black icing and No. 1.5 tip. Flood the udder using flesh icing and No. 1.5 tip.

5

Flood the body using white icing and No. 1.5 tip. While the icing is wet, pipe the spot, remaining hooves, and tail using black icing and No. 1.5 tip.

6

Pipe the horns and snout using flesh icing and No. 2 tip. To make the snout, pipe a large dot and immediately pipe a second dot next to it. Let them blend. While the icing is wet, use accent tweezers to add 2 black nonpareils as nostrils.

7

Pipe the hair tress using brown icing and No. 14 tip. Using a paintbrush, apply pink petal dust on the cheeks. Use a fine black edible marker to draw the eyes.

Wish Upon a Star

The sparkling tail on the star gives this cookie a real personality. This theme for babies can also be used for a baby shower or cute gender reveal if you adjust the color of the background to suit your theme. *MS*

SUPPLIES

- 2¾-in (7-cm) fluted edge circle cookie cutter
- Smaller round cookie cutter
- Yellow edible marker
- 3 piping bags and couplers
- Piping tips (Nos. 1.5, 2, 3)
- Accent tweezers
- Black edible pearls
- Yellow edible glitter
- Round No. 4 or No. 5 paintbrush
- Pink petal dust
- Toothpick
- White edible airbrush color
- Royal icing:

Royal blue (honey consistency)

Egg yellow (meringue consistency)

White (meringue consistency)

1

Choose a basic cookie recipe on page 7, and make a batch of cookies using a fluted edge circle cutter. Allow the cookies to cool completely before decorating. Use a smaller round cutter and yellow edible marker to trace a circle on the cookie as a guide for the sky. Use royal blue icing and No. 3 tip to outline and flood the circle. Allow to dry.

2

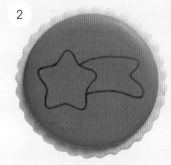

Trace the shooting star onto the blue icing using the yellow edible marker and the provided template (see pages 134–139).

3

Outline and flood the star with egg yellow icing and No. 2 tip. While the icing is wet, use accent tweezers to add 2 black edible pearls as eyes. Use the same icing to decorate the fluted edge of the cookie with yellow dots. Allow to dry.

4

Pipe the tail with the same color and consistency. Immediately apply edible glitter to the tail. Add white icing dots between the yellow ones around the fluted edge using No. 1.5 tip.

5

Using a paintbrush, apply pink petal dust to the cheeks. Dip a toothpick in white edible airbrush color and paint a small dot on each cheek. Use a black edible marker to draw a smile. Finally, pipe random small white dots over the sky background using No. 1.5 tip.

Fingerprint Flower

Fingerprint flower cookies make a great gift for Mother's Day and they are easy to design, too.
If you're baking these for grandma, get the kids to help, as it's just like finger painting! *NK*

SUPPLIES

- Fancy plaque cutter
- 2 piping bags
- Palette
- Violet food color
- Blue food color
- A piece of sponge
- Royal icing (regular consistency):
  White
  Green

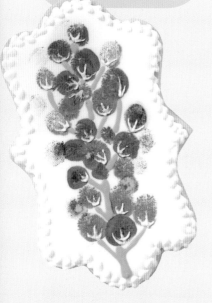

1

Choose a basic cookie recipe on page 7, and make a batch of cookies using a fancy plaque cutter. Allow the cookies to cool completely before decorating. Prepare the piping bags by cutting a 1–2-mm hole for piping and a 3-mm hole for flooding. Outline and flood the cookie with white icing. Allow to dry completely.

2

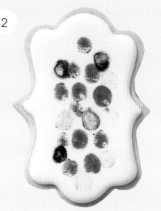

Drop some violet and blue food colors on a palette. Using a sponge, dab a little violet color on your finger and make fingerprints on the cookie.

3

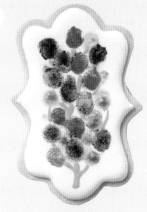

Do the same with blue food color. Pipe the flower stems using green icing.

4

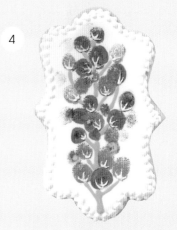

Pipe white lines on the bottom of every flower using white icing. Pipe a border around the cookie using white icing. Allow to dry completely.

Perfume Bottle

Perhaps you're buying mom a bottle of perfume for her Mother's Day gift. If not, these make a great alternative to the real thing—and best of all, you can eat this one! *NK*

SUPPLIES

- Ring cookie cutter
- 3 piping bags
- Paintbrush
- Gold food color
- Accent tweezers
- White sugar pearls
- Satin bows
- Royal icing (regular consistency):
  Gold yellow
  Brown
  White

1

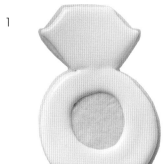

Choose a basic cookie recipe on page 7, and make a batch of cookies using a ring cutter. Before baking, trim the bases. Allow the cookies to cool completely before decorating. Prepare the piping bags by cutting a 1–2-mm hole for piping and a 3-mm hole for flooding. Use gold yellow icing to outline and flood the bottle, leaving a space in the middle.

2

Outline the bottle then pipe lines on the top of the bottle using gold yellow icing. Allow to dry.

3

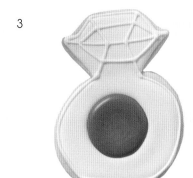

Flood the middle of the bottle using brown icing. Allow to dry completely.

4

Paint the circle with gold food color. Using white icing, pipe a floral pattern around the circle. Use accent tweezers to place sugar pearls in the center. Pipe lines down the sides using gold yellow icing. Glue a satin bow on the bottle.

Hat

I love polka-dot patterns on everything but especially on hats! These colorful cookies will put a smile on Mom's face this Mother's Day. *NK*

SUPPLIES

- Hat cookie cutter
- 4 piping bags
- Swirl rose transfers (see page 17)
- Royal icing (regular consistency):
  - White
  - Tan
  - Black
  - Red

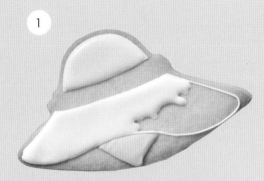

1 Choose a basic cookie recipe on page 7, and make a batch of cookies using a hat cutter. Allow the cookies to cool completely before decorating. Prepare the piping bags by cutting a 1–2-mm hole for piping and a 3-mm hole for flooding. Prepare the swirl roses in advance (see page 17). Outline and flood the lower and upper parts of the hat with white icing. Pipe the lower part of the face with tan icing.

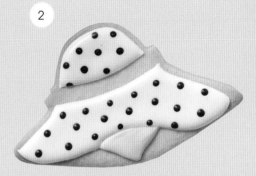

2 While the icing is wet, pipe black dots on the hat, working evenly across the lower and upper sections. Allow to dry completely.

3 Pipe the ribbon with black icing. While it is wet, stick the rose transfer on the right side of the hat. Pipe tiny dots with red icing on either side of the rose. Add white leaves with white icing. Pipe lips on the face with red icing. Allow to dry completely.

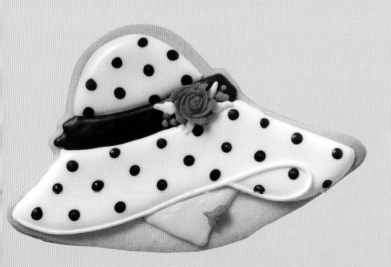

Whimsical Roses

These pretty cookies might look complicated, but they are actually fairly simple to make. I use pink as the accent color here, but you can adjust the colors to suit your preference. *NK*

SUPPLIES

- Round fluted edge cutter
- 5 piping bags
- Piping tip (No. 65s)
- Metal skewer or toothpick
- Royal icing (regular consistency):
  White
  Dark and light pink
  Leaf and dark green

1 Choose a basic cookie recipe on page 7, and make a batch of cookies using a round fluted edge cutter. Allow the cookies to cool completely before decorating. Prepare the piping bags that don't require a tip by cutting a 1–2-mm hole for piping and a 3-mm hole for flooding. Outline and flood the cookie using white icing.

2 While the icing is wet, pipe dots on the bottom half of the cookie using dark pink and light pink icing (see picture).

3 Pipe leaf green dots among the pink dots. Using a metal skewer or toothpick, drag through the dots to make leaves. Pipe tiny pink dots near the leaves using light pink icing. Allow to dry completely.

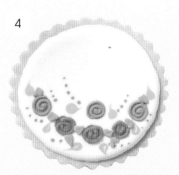

4 Make a swirl on top of each big pink dot using the same pink for each dot. Pipe tiny leaves using dark green icing and No. 65s tip.

5 Pipe a border around the cookie with alternate pink and white dots. Allow to dry completely.

Dad's Tie

These cookies will be a welcome gift for dads and grandpas on Father's Day. I use the wet-on-wet technique (see page 17) for this design. *NK*

SUPPLIES

- Tie cookie cutter
- 5 piping bags
- Metal skewer or toothpick
- Royal icing (regular consistency):
  Brown
  Yellow
  Pink
  White
  Fuchsia

1

Choose a basic cookie recipe on page 7, and make a batch of cookies using a tie cutter. Allow the cookies to cool completely before decorating. Prepare the piping bags by cutting a 1–2-mm hole for piping and a 3-mm hole for flooding. Outline and flood the tie with brown icing.

2

Pipe oblique lines on the tie using yellow, pink, white, and fuchsia icing (see picture).

3

Using a metal skewer or toothpick, drag it up and down through the cookie to create a colorful pattern.

4

Outline the cookies with brown icing and allow to dry completely.

Grill

Plenty of dads love grilling, so these cookies will be a great surprise for Father's Day. Take your time with the detailing, as the finished design can look very realistic. *NK*

SUPPLIES

- Grill cookie cutter
- 3 piping bags
- Royal icing (regular consistency):
  Red
  White
  Black

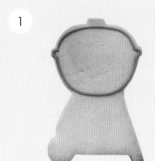

1 Choose a basic cookie recipe on page 7, and make a batch of cookies using a grill cutter. Allow the cookies to cool completely before decorating. Prepare the piping bags by cutting a 1–2-mm hole for piping and a 3-mm hole for flooding. Outline the main part of the grill using red icing.

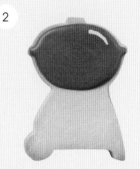

2 Flood the grill with red icing. While the icing is wet, pipe a reflection on the right side of the grill using white icing.

3 Pipe the grill handle and legs using black icing (see picture). Pipe the wheel with white icing and pipe a black icing dot in the center of it.

4 Pipe 2 red lines in the middle of the grill for the lid using red icing. Allow to dry completely.

Cool Pop

I use sky blue royal icing as the feature color on this cookie so it looks ice cool! But of course, you can change the color if you like. *MS*

SUPPLIES

- Cool pop cookie cutter
- 5 piping bags and couplers
- Piping tips (Nos. 1.5, 2, 3)
- Accent tweezers
- Edible black pearls (⅛ in/4 mm)
- Royal icing:
  Brown (honey consistency)
  Ivory (meringue consistency)
  Sky blue (honey consistency)
  White (honey consistency)
  Pink (honey consistency)

1. Choose a basic cookie recipe on page 7, and make a batch of cookies using a cool pop cutter. Allow the cookies to cool completely before decorating.

2. Outline and flood the mustache using brown icing and No. 3 tip.

3. Outline and flood the popsicle stick using ivory icing and No. 2 tip. Allow to dry.

4. Pipe the upper popsicle area using sky blue icing and No. 2 tip. While the icing is wet, pipe lines using white icing (see picture). Use accent tweezers to add black pearls for eyes. Pipe 2 dots as cheeks using pink icing and No. 1.5 tip.

5. Fill the lower area of the popsicle using sky blue icing. Allow to dry completely.

6. Pipe some lines onto the mustache using brown icing and No. 1.5 tip. Allow to dry completely.

TIPS & TRICKS

Don't worry if the icing details in the popsicle do not merge completely—that's the intention.

Superhero Dad

Dads will love receiving these star-shaped cookies on Father's Day as a show of appreciation. There are a few finer details on this design, but older kids can help with most of the decorating.
MS

SUPPLIES

- Superhero plaque cookie cutter
- 4 piping bags and couplers
- Piping tips (Nos. 1.5, 2, 3)
- Silver edible marker
- Airbrush
- Orange edible airbrush color
- Accent tweezers
- White star sprinkles
- Royal icing:
  Red (meringue consistency)
  Yellow (10-second consistency)
  Black (honey consistency)
  Yellow (meringue consistency)

1. Choose a basic cookie recipe on page 7, and make a batch of cookies using a superhero plaque cutter. Allow the cookies to cool completely before decorating.
2. Outline the cookie using red icing and No. 3 tip. Allow to dry completely.
3. Flood the cookie using yellow icing (10-second consistency) and No. 3 tip. Allow to dry completely.
4. Trace the dad using a silver edible marker and the provided template (see pages 134–139).
5. Airbrush the plaque edges using orange edible airbrush color. Allow to dry completely.
6. Outline and flood the dad silhouette using black icing and No. 1.5 tip. Allow to dry completely.
7. Trace the tie using the silver edible marker and the provided template (see pages 134–139).
8. Pipe the tie using yellow royal icing (meringue consistency) and No. 1.5 tip.
9. Use tweezers and a little icing to glue white star sprinkles on the background. Allow to dry completely.

TIPS & TRICKS

As an alternative to the template, you can make the tie as a royal icing transfer (see page 16), and glue it while the silhouette is still wet.

Templates

Basketball, p. 24

Soccer Ball, p. 24

Pirate, p. 26

Ballerina, p. 28

Dinosaur, p. 31

Sweetheart, p. 53

Leprechaun, p. 57

Chick, p. 62

Jack-o-Lantern, p. 76

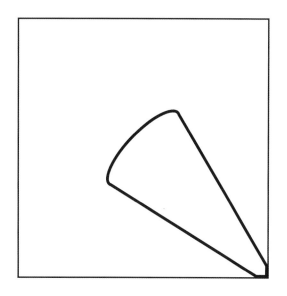

Party Popper, p. 100

Silhouette, p. 105

Cow Jumped Over the Moon, p. 120

Wish Upon a Star, p. 121

Superhero Dad, p. 132

Suppliers & Resources

Amazon
www.amazon.com

Ann Clark
www.annclarkcookiecutters.com

Bake it Pretty
www.bakeitpretty.com

Bakers Nook
www.shopbakersnook.com

Bakers Stock
www.bakersstock.com

Broadway Panhandler
www.broadwaypanhandler.com

Cake Connection
www.cakeconnection.com

Cake Craft Shop
www.cakecraftshop.co.uk

Cake Craft World
www.cakecraftworld.co.uk

Cakes, Cookies & Crafts
www.cakescookiesandcraftsshop.co.uk

Chapix Cookies
www.chapixcookies.com

Cheap Cookie Cutters
www.cheapcookiecutters.com

Copper Gifts
www.coppergifts.com

Fancy Flours
www.fancyflours.com

Global Sugar Art
www.globalsugarart.com

H.O. Foose Tinsmithing Co.
www.foosecookiecutters.com

JB Cookie Cutters
www.jbcookiecutters.com

Karen's Cookies
www.karenscookies.net

King Arthur Flour
www.kingarthurflour.com

Kitchen Krafts
www.kitchenkrafts.com

Kopykake
www.kopykake.com

Lakeland
www.lakeland.co.uk

Planet Bake
www.planetbake.co.uk

Rainbow Dust
www.rainbowdust.co.uk

Squires Kitchen
www.squires-shop.com

Sugar Nice
www.sugarnice.co.uk

Sur La Table
www.surlatable.com

Sweet Art Factory
www.sweetartfactory.com

The Cookie Cutter Company
www.cookiecuttercompany.com

The Cookie Cutter Shop
www.thecookiecuttershop.com

Totally Sugar Crafts
www.totallysugarcrafts.co.uk

Williams-Sonoma
www.williams-sonoma.com

Wilton
www.wilton.com

NADIA YOUTUBE CHANNEL:
http://tinyurl.com/nzr3sjb

MYRIAM YOUTUBE CHANNEL:
www.youtube.com/user/ChapixCookies

 NADIA FACEBOOK:
www.facebook.com/NadiaMLB

MYRIAM FACEBOOK:
www.facebook.com/ChapixCookies

Chapix Cookies

A number of Myriam's designs in the book use cookie cutters that have been created by Chapix Cookies. You can view and order these cutters by visiting the website **www.chapixcookies.com**

Index